Tales from
WWII
You Probably Never Heard Before

ZED MERRILL

CLASSIC DAY
PUBLISHING

Seattle, Washington
Portland, Oregon
Denver, Colorado
Vancouver, B.C.
Scottsdale, Arizona
Minneapolis, Minnesota

Classic Day Publishing
Pier: Julie's Landing
2100 Westlake Avenue North
Seattle, Washington 98109
800-328-4348
www.classicdaypublishing.com

TABLE OF CONTENTS

DEDICATION

It would be impossible to list all of those who played an important part in my life that would eventually lead to this book. To attempt to do so, I'm afraid, would get me in a heap of trouble, because I'm sure after the volumes of pages it would take me to list names I would most certainly, unintentionally of course, leave somebody out. I could perhaps have a brave go at it, then fall back on the perfect escape hatch reserved for those who are approaching the 80-years-of-age zone at the speed of light and simply claim, "I can't remember," and maybe get away with it. I think I'll go with that. But then if I expect to go home for dinner I better at least go with the "A" group.

I'm indebted to my father, who once advised me to select whatever I wanted to do in life and go for it with patience and perseverance. So that's what I did, because I really wanted to do all those things I had in mind. And to my mother who thought some of the things I did were funny when they probably weren't, but nevertheless gave me a measure of confidence. Her one regret, and mine too, is that I never learned how to play the piano.

But how are you going to convince a twelve year old kid who would rather be playing baseball and going to the movies.

I give special thanks to my five wonderful children, Cindy, Sally, Libby, Zed Jr. and Tawny, all of whom were great kids and who would even become greater adults in providing their mom and dad with horizon-to-horizon grandkids, who in turn are now bringing forth the great grandkids.

And thank you most certainly to my wife Norma, who I first met in a high school journalism class back in 1941. She had spilled ink all over a poster I was making. Was that love at first sight or what? For more than sixty years she has supported everything I wanted to do. Even when those things went a little south at times.

To this special "A" group I dedicate this effort.

ACKNOWLEDGMENTS

Particular appreciation is due to the following, who made this work possible, both directly and indirectly.

Mark Heinsoo, editor of *Northwest Senior Life* for suggesting I share these stories by writing a column for his publication; William Brosseau, whose more than 25 years of excellent camera and editing work greatly contributed to the success of my WWII video productions; C.M. Graham and his book *Under the Samurai Sword*, that encouraged me to finally do one myself; Elliott Wolf of Peanut Butter Publishing who helped me get through the mechanics of this thing, and to my wife Norma who for more than half-a-century has said to me "you ought to write a book."

The others are C.A. Lloyd, Chairman of the U.S. Navy Armed Guard WWII Veterans Association; Lyle Dupra, author of *We Delivered*; Don McCombs and Fred L. Worth's excellent reference book, *Strange and Fascinating Facts.*; The Glencannon Press for approval to refer to their book, *Nightmare at Bari*; Tom Hobson who helped me put the commas and periods in the right places; to the libraries and their wealth of pages that told me what I was looking for, and in doing so revealed surprises I wasn't looking for, and to the unique World War II generation who went off to war without question, either on the battlefield or on the home front, to save our freedom at a time when America's hours were the darkest. Without their personal contributions this book wouldn't have been possible.

And a special thanks to those who supplied photos: Robert Potts, Mrs. Roland "Spec" Martin, Walt Larsen, James Burke, Norman and Solang Langelier, the Bomber Restaurant in Milwaukie, Oregon, and David Marty for the cover design.

INTRODUCTION

I guess you would have to say the idea for this book began back in the winter of 1996. It started when my wife, Norma, pulled up behind a car at a stop light, and while she was waiting for the light to change, she noticed the car's rear bumper sticker: "U.S. Navy Armed Guard WWII Veteran." She couldn't believe what she was seeing. I had served in that outfit, and for nearly sixty years since the war had ended we had heard or read nothing about the Navy Armed Guard. Even during the war, little or nothing was written about this obscure branch of the Navy.

As the light changed, and fearing the driver of the car in front of her would exit on to the freeway a few blocks away, she began honking her horn until the car pulled over into a bank parking lot. The driver got out and walked back to her car somewhat shaken and wondering what he had done wrong. "Nothing." she replied, "It's just that my husband was in the Navy Armed Guard during the war. Where did you get that bumper sticker?"

One thing led to another, and within one month we were in St. Louis with a camera crew at a Navy Armed Guard reunion interviewing twenty four veterans. Three months later we released a one-hour documentary titled *Forgotten Valor*, which became the only filmed record of the Navy Armed Guard during World War II. It would later win an international award and help bring about the Armed Guard finally being placed in the U.S. Congressional Record for their unsung WWII achievements.

Other WWII documentaries followed, and along the way I began receiving letters, emails and telephone calls from veterans from every branch of the services. This also included the people who had stayed home to do their part to aid the war effort. They all had stories to tell. And during my research for the videos I began uncovering interesting little-known stories behind the big stories that had been public record for more than half-a-century. Mark Heinsoo, editor of *Northwest Senior Life*, heard about this collection and asked me if I would share some of these stories in a monthly column. This triggered more people contacting me about their war experiences. It wasn't long before I realized I was writing a book.

Today, as I prepare for future documentaries about the war, my research continues to reveal more intriguing and unknown facts behind the main story. And every now and then a letter will come, or I'll receive a telephone call from someone who has a personal story they feel should be told. You could sense a quiet tone of urgency about it; as if should their story not be put into some kind of record now it would be lost forever. After all, that generation, the one Tom Brokaw so correctly labeled "The Greatest Generation," is disappearing faster than we realize.

These are some of those stories. They are incredible, to say the least. But then those times were incredible, the likes we hopefully will never see again.

PERSEVERANCE

As I was preparing to produce *No Way Back*, a video documentary based on U.S. Merchant Marine prisoners-of-war, a veteran mariner from Mississippi contacted me about a fellow seaman who had survived one of the most extraordinary war experiences of which I had ever heard.

The seaman's name was Jack Smith.

In 1942, the United States was running endless convoys of war supplies from the U.S. to England and then over the North Atlantic Ocean into the port of Murmansk, Russia. The Germans, at that time, were winning the war against Russia and this was the only route — barely open — to get help to the Russians. In addition to the American convoys, the U.S. was also supplying the Russians with many of the cargo ships for their own use. Some of these ships were the famous Liberty Ships, which most Russian seamen weren't trained to operate. Enter Jack Smith.

Smith and two of his mariner shipmates volunteered to journey on one particular Liberty Ship to Russia and train their Russian counterparts on how to operate the various loading and unloading equipment. They did so, however, on one condition. That they be paid in U.S. dollars and not worthless Russian rubles. The Russian authorities agreed.

After a treacherous voyage that took weeks, surviving deadly German U-boat attacks and the frozen North Atlantic seas, they finally arrived in ice-bound Murmansk near the Arctic Circle.

But when Smith and his buddies went ashore to collect their wages in U.S. funds the Russians backed down. The three Americans raised such a ruckus that they were bound and thrown on the back of a truck and sent off into the wilderness to a Russian civilian concentration camp. The Russians, supposedly our allies, claimed they never saw the young seaman. They were reported as missing or possibly killed from one of the daily German air raids.

Within a few weeks, Smith escaped alone from the Russian prison camp and made his way north across the frozen wasteland into what was at the time, unknown to him, German occupied territory. After several narrow escapes from German patrols he came upon a caravan of nomads carrying furs and pelts on the backs of reindeer. For several days he journeyed with the friendly nomads as they moved west toward Finland.

Then, early one morning, a German patrol came upon the caravan and started searching the fur-draped reindeer for weapons. Finding nothing, the patrol moved on. For one nightmarish hour, Smith was miraculously concealed from the Germans by being strapped to the underbelly of a fur-covered, and very patient, reindeer. Weeks later, he left the caravan at the Finnish border and took off on foot across snow fields and through forests, carefully eluding those who worked as "bounty hunters" for both the Germans and Russians.

Half frozen and starving, Smith wandered across the northern part of Sweden, climbing mountains and crossing endless and desolate ice-covered fields, eating garbage and finding shelter in barns and behind fallen trees. With some friendly assistance, he was guided to the Norwegian underground where they in turn smuggled him passed German forces into a small fishing village on the shore of the North Sea.

He was then smuggled aboard a small fishing boat that risked a dangerous crossing of the rough seas to help him escape to Scotland. But the voyage was not without incident. A crew of a German warship boarded the fishing vessel off the Norwegian coast to search for anything suspicious. They came up empty handed. Once again, Smith had escaped the Germans by hiding below deck covered up with hundreds of fish.

As the fishing boat reached the shores of Scotland, Smith bid his Norwegian friends goodbye and swam the last few hundred yards to shore. Within minutes he was stopped by a British patrol. With no identification, and coming ashore rather suspiciously, he was marched away to a local jail. He was now under arrest as a German spy.

Eventually, through confirmation from the U.S. Maritime Service, Smith was released from the British prison and cleared of spy charges. After a few months he caught an American ship back to New York where he signed on for another ship and went right back to Russia over the same hellish North Atlantic, once again fending off relentless German submarine and air attacks. He did it not once, but several times.

The war finally ended, but not for Jack Smith. He went back to sea again, this time on ships carrying war supplies to our fighting forces in Korea. Then when the Vietnam War happened, guess who was working on the merchant ships that sailed to support our forces in that battle zone?

On June 23, 1997, Jack Smith passed away. After more than half-a-century of searching, Smith was never able to find out what happened to his two shipmates who were left behind in the Russian prison camp.

WE REGRET TO INFORM YOU...

In November of 2001, I released a video documentary titled *The Last Day of Innocence* which centered around one typical small American town and how it was affected by the Pearl Harbor attack on December 7, 1941. I chose Albany, Oregon.

Among the people recommended to be interviewed was Rolland "Spec" Martin, an Albany native who enlisted in the navy in 1937 and who had been stationed aboard the battleship *West Virginia* based at Pearl Harbor. The big battle wagon was destroyed that day along with almost all of the U.S. Pacific fleet. The surprise attack killed over 3,000 military and civilian personnel. Hundreds were killed and missing on the *West Virginia* alone.

Martin talked briefly about the attack, how people on the home front responded to the war effort, and then following the interview he drove home some 40 miles away. It wasn't until an hour later that one of the other people being interviewed casually mentioned what an incredible story Martin must have told. I was puzzled because what Martin said was interesting, but nothing really out of the ordinary.

Then I was told. I telephoned Martin the next day and he graciously agreed to return again a week later to tell this amazing story.

Several days after the attack, the navy department notified Martin's parents in Albany with the standard, "We regret to inform you...." letter that their son had been killed on the *West Virginia*. The local newspaper ran a big story with his picture headlining the tragedy. Martin's mother suffered a stroke.

Two months later, the navy department suddenly discovered through all the confusion caused by the attack that Martin had actually survived the bombing and was now stateside at the San Diego Navy Base.

Another telegram was quickly sent to the Albany Western Union office, whereupon a boy was sent out on his bicycle to deliver

the message of the good news to the Martin family. The messenger boy, however, went to the wrong house, found nobody home, and so he threw the telegram away.

As far as Mr. and Mrs. Martin were concerned, their son had been killed two months prior at Pearl Harbor. In the meantime, young Martin became worried that his parents hadn't responded to the telegram. After

He was one of the first casualties of WWII at Pearl Harbor. Or was he?

awhile, he decided to call home. Placing a long-distance call in 1942 would often take hours, sometimes days, to get through. When he finally made the connection, his father answered and almost went into shock. Young Martin asked his father to send him $75.00 so he could come home on leave. His father agreed, hung up and immediately called the Albany Police.

Instead of wiring the $75.00 to his son, the elder Martin enlisted the aid of the Chief of Police to trap and catch the imposter. At the time, it was not uncommon for families to receive telephone calls, or telegrams from those posing as their sons to collect money, when in fact they had already been killed in action or listed as missing. To the Martin family, this call seemed very suspicious.

The elder Martin and the Chief of Police climbed aboard a train at Albany and made the long two day trip to San Diego. When the two confronted the so-called imposter at the designated place where he was to receive the money, they stood stunned as young Martin walked up to his father and embraced him.

When the war ended, Rolland "Spec" Martin returned to Albany and became a doctor. On December 7, 2001 he journeyed back to Pearl Harbor and attended the 60th anniversary of that tragic event, and was reunited with his shipmates who had also survived the *West Virginia*.

THE CHANGING STORY

During World War II, there were many celebrities who gave up lucrative movie careers to enlist in the military and fight to help save democracy. A good many of them could have been deferred by claiming they would serve their country best by making moral-boosting movies and entertaining servicemen. The majority of them, however, chose to enlist. Among the many that went off to war were James Stewart, Tyrone Power, Douglas Fairbanks, Jr., Clark Gable and Leslie Howard.

It's Leslie Howard's tragic story that kept changing until the right one was finally told.

Howard was a well-known British actor who became a big star here in America during the 1930's. His smash-hit performance on Broadway in *The Petrified Forest* sent him to Hollywood where he starred in the movie version. This led to *Of Human Bondage* opposite Bette Davis, which in turn led to his leading role in *Intermezzo* with a young Ingrid Bergman. When they cast for *Gone With the Wind*, Howard was the overwhelming choice to play the important role of Ashley Wilkes. The movie, which was released in 1939, is considered by movie critics to be one of the greatest movies ever made.

Before Pearl Harbor brought the United States into the war, Howard put his movie career on hold and returned to his native England and joined the Royal Air Force to fight against Nazi Germany. In June of 1943, Howard was listed as being shot down by enemy planes in a British Spitfire. Apparently this sounded more heroic than what really happened. Later, his story was revised to one of him being on a bomber that was jumped by a squadron of German fighters. Near the end of the war the true story finally came out, and also the true extent of the tragedy: Howard's death could have been avoided.

Howard was aboard a BOAC 777, a British Overseas Airways flight from Algiers to London, when German fighters attacked and shot down the airliner over the Bay of Biscay. One of the passengers on that plane, the Germans thought, was British Prime Minister Winston Churchill. Actually it was Alfred Chenfalls, a double for Churchill who the British used on many occasions during the war to deceive enemy intelligence.

Just prior to the attack, the British had secretly broken the German code and knew beforehand that the plane was going to be attacked. Rather than tip their hand to the Germans that they had cracked their code, the British decided not to warn the plane's crew about what was going to happen. As a result, no British fighters were sent out to intercept the attacking German aircraft.

The plane, with one of the era's greatest movie actors, went down with no survivors, and the Germans thought they had actually killed Winston Churchill.

FROM MOVIE QUEEN SCIENTIST
TO A NAZI MICKEY MOUSE

When I started producing World War II video documentaries in 1996, my goal was to tell stories about little-known events that helped shape our victory, and to reveal heroic sacrifices made by individuals and military units that had been forgotten on the history pages of the war.

But the fascinating content of the hundreds of letters I received was something I hadn't expected. Many came from WWII historians who sent me documented evidence that particular unknown things and events had actually occurred. Others came from individuals who had experienced unbelievable and sometimes humorous situations.

Here are just a few of these fascinating gems.

The name of the inventor of an important torpedo guidance system during the war was finally revealed after the inventor's death. Her name was Hedy Lamarr, one of Hollywood's all-time most glamorous actresses.

Just before the outbreak of the war in Europe in 1939, Germany claimed 230,000 square miles of Antarctica at the South Pole. Whatever they had in mind as a military base that far away remains a mystery.

In one Japanese prisoner-of-war camp, an American GI tells how his captors would line up outside the barbed wire compound and chant these insults at the American captives: "To hell with Roosevelt, to hell with Babe Ruth and to hell with Roy Acuff."

Would you believe there was a guy who served in the U.S. Navy during WWII by the name of William Patrick Hitler? You wouldn't? Well he did, and he was the son of Adolf Hitler's half-brother, which would make him a nephew to the German dictator. Following the war he thought it might be wise to change his name. Oh, really?

Pappy Boyington was one of our top fighter pilots. During the war he shot down 28 Japanese planes and was awarded the Medal of Honor. Kept secret, however, was his shooting down by mistake of an American pilot from a small town in Oregon. The victim, who survived the ordeal, decided not to reveal himself 25 years later during a Boyington autograph event in fear that it might embarrass the war ace.

On November 26, 1943, a B-17 bomber with the name of *Murder, Inc.* was shot down over Germany. The crew bailed out and was immediately captured. Painted on the backs of their flight jackets was *Murder, Inc.*, of which the Germans gleefully took advantage by using it as propaganda to show their people, much to the amusement of the captured Americans, that the United States was using gangsters as bomber crews.

Whenever a U.S. submarine returned to base, the navy band would stand on the dock and strike up a rousing welcome. No, it wasn't *Anchors Aweigh*. It was *Roll Out the Barrel*.

A German soldier who was part of Hitler's military guard, and who later became a US citizen, said the German dictator's private armored train that he helped guard was named *Amerika*.

The term GI used throughout the war was generally understood to stand for Government Issue. Not so. It actually began when army supply clerks listed garbage cans as GI for galvanized iron.

When Germany was preparing to launch an invasion into a small European country in 1939, they realized their road maps were 30 years old. The assault was delayed until they contacted one of the country's travel agencies and received back an updated packet of the usual tourist attractions and road maps. The information was extremely helpful in their swift and decisive defeat of the country.

One of the most complete all-Allied efforts of the war occurred on October 6, 1944 when the *U-168* sunk a German submarine. The *U-168* was a Dutch submarine, built by the British, based in Australia, and operated by the United States.

The number one march used by Hitler and the Nazi party to rally German audiences into a frenzy was none other than the Harvard University fight song.

Guess what one of Germany's leading war aces, Adolf Galland, had painted on the side of his ME109? No, not a Swastika. It was Mickey Mouse.

THE RAREST OF GIFTS

One of the most dangerous battlefields of World War II was the North Atlantic. Over these treacherous seas that ran from England up to the Arctic Circle and into the northern ports of Murmansk and Archangel, Russia, Allied convoys delivered essential war supplies to help Russia hold on against the onslaught of Nazi Germany. The price that was paid by the allies in lives and shipping, especially for the United States, was staggering.

Having to endure the constant menace of the German U-Boats was one nightmare. Being ice-bound in these barren, bombed-out Russian ports with little food and little heat was quite another. Trapped for months by the frigid Arctic ice and the daily German air raids had become a way of life.

Norman Langelier was a U.S. Navy Armed Guard gunner on a Liberty Ship that made it safely into Archangel. He vowed if his ship could make it back to England through the deadly German *Wolfpacks* that were waiting for them off the northern coast of Norway, he would bring home a special and rare gift for his mother: a priceless Siberian fur piece. He would get it for her no matter what the cost.

After meeting secretly with a local Russian youth, and expressing his desire to obtain such a fur, Langelier loaded himself down with cigarettes and candy bars and set out following his young guide through the snow-covered and bomb-charred streets. Temperatures were well below zero.

Upon reaching the outskirts of the city, the pursuit continued through acres of frozen wasteland, across ice-jammed streams, and through several miles of thick forest. Like his youthful escort, Langelier was prepared for the Russian cold — perhaps even more so. He had on long thermal underwear, a heavy fur lined coat, cap, gloves, wool socks and a pair of warm knee-high boots. The deadly cold was beginning to creep through, but the American sailor trudged on relentlessly in quest of his mission.

Finally a small cabin appeared. Upon entering, Langelier was met by two large, bearded Russians sitting behind a table that displayed several beautiful fur pieces. One priceless looking fur in particular caught his eye. He offered the Russians the cigarettes and then the candy. They shook their heads "no." One Russian tugged at the American's collar where a piece of his thermal underwear was peeking out beneath his clothes. Langelier first said, "No," but then agreed to give them up since he figured he had another pair anyway, back on board ship.

Now naked and shivering after stripping off his long underwear, he was in the process of re-dressing when one of the other Russians pointed at his wool socks. Why not? he thought. He had two more pair back at the ship. Next came his fur-lined cap and before he could get his gloves back on they had taken those too. No way was the coat or boots going to be part of the deal. No way! But his mother back home had to have this rare and beautiful fur.

So the boots went on the table. But only in exchange for something the Russians might have that resembled shoes so he wouldn't leave there barefooted. The deal was struck and Langelier left hurriedly with his coat luckily still on his back and the fur tucked safely inside.

The long trek back through falling snow and icy wind was unbearable. Freezing and numb, the determined sailor staggered half dazed back through the forest, over the frozen streams and across the endless barren wasteland.

The frozen wasteland of northern Russia couldn't keep this sailor from trading almost everything he had for a rare Siberian gift for his mother.

On the edge of the city, he stumbled into a small Russian army camp. He was given a blanket, where he huddled outside next to a fire, sipped some hot-but-tasteless soup, and then slept fitfully in a tent until daybreak. He was then dragged on a sled through town and dumped at the pier where his ship was docked. Somewhat delirious, he crawled his way up the gangway and into his cabin, still clutching the fur beneath his coat. For some time after that he laid in his bunk with a fever, fearing he might not make it through.

Months later, fully recovered and having also escaped the clutches of the German submarines, Langelier set foot in New York Harbor. He had survived an almost unbearable ordeal to obtain a precious and priceless Siberian fur for his mother. He couldn't believe what he had actually gone through. He might have died. But to him it had been worth it.

When Langelier arrived home on leave in Rhode Island, he proudly presented the fur to his mother. She wept when she heard what he had gone though for her. She would cherish the gift forever. Wherever she went, she was envied by those who saw the fur and congratulated for having such a loving and devoted son.

Beaming with pride, she and her son took the fur to a respected fur dealer to have such a valuable piece appraised. The furrier inspected it closely and then looked up at them both.

"Well, the news I have for you," the furrier said, "is that this is probably one of the finest dog furs I've ever seen."

LACEY'S LADY

What you are about to read is an incredible mission of a particular World War II B-17 bomber. It's not about it dropping a payload of bombs on an enemy munitions plant, and then being overwhelmed by attacking enemy planes as it heroically limped back to safety on a wing and a prayer. You know, the kind of war story the movies made over and over again. As a matter of fact, this amazing mission, and where the B-17 finally landed, is one of those tales Hollywood would say was too improbable to be passed off as being true.

But it is true. And it all started with an all-night poker game....two years *after* the war had ended.

It was 1947, and Art Lacey of Milwaukie, Oregon was celebrating his birthday by playing poker with his old friend Bob Haas from Vancouver, Washington, which is across the Columbia River from Portland, Oregon. During the course of the game, Haas bet Lacey five dollars that he couldn't go out and buy a B-17 and fly it back to Oregon. Lacey took the bet and flew the very next day to Oklahoma City where he knew hundreds of WWII bombers were in a "graveyard" at the nearby Altus Air Base.

To the utter astonishment of the base commander, Lacey dolled out nearly $14,000 in cash for one of the warbirds, and informed the officer he planned to fly it back to Oregon. Thinking perhaps Lacy was an ex-war pilot, with thousands of hours in bombing missions over enemy territory, the deal was closed. The truth was that Lacey had only eight hours in the air,

17

The B-17 Bomber that made an astonishing flight to a final resting place all because of a $5.00 bet.

and that was in a little two-seat private plane. He knew absolutely nothing about flying a B-17.

After spending five days and nights pouring over flight manuals, taxiing several times up and down the runway, Lacey was ready to try a take off. But he was required to have a co-pilot. He got around this obstacle with the help of a farm boy who helped him prep the plane. It seems the boy was the son of a dressmaker who willingly sold Lacey a mannequin, which in turn became the co-pilot wearing Lacy's cap. It fooled the Altus tower, and Lacey took off down the runway for a practice flight. He circled around the base easily, then decided to land. Then it happened.

The landing gear froze and Lacy became terrified. Being a novice flyer he couldn't think fast enough how he might correct the problem. He had no choice but to put it down on the ground wheels up. He hit the runway sliding, taking out a parked B-17, ripping off a wing and spilling gas everywhere. He walked away and immediately headed straight back, wanting to purchase another B-17. In an effort probably intended to get him off the base as quickly as possible, Lacey was sold another bomber for only $1,500. Then with the help of two pilot friends who flew down from Oregon, Lacey and his small crew finally took off for the Northwest.

Flying as low as possible, in order to follow railroad tracks and highways in an effort to read signs to guide them back to the Portland area, they encountered blizzards and ice storms, and barely missing a mountain top. Once they flew nearly 100 miles off course. Then when Lacey took the bomber up to 22,000 feet to get above the bad weather, they all began to suffer the painful effects from the lack of oxygen. Adding to this, they couldn't land for gas in Bend, Oregon because the airport was under two feet of snow.

One time while Lacey was at the controls, and staying above the clouds, he was reminded by one of his co-pilots that this was a good way to get lost since they were flying by the seat of their pants. Lacey was warned he could lose his license. His response was, "Don't worry, I don't have a license.

Thirty-six hours after leaving Oklahoma, having made two stops along the way, but now running on gas fumes, Lacey brought the B-17 into a small airport outside of Portland. But it was not without incident. He barely escaped a head-on collision with a small aircraft approaching the runway from the opposite direction. After all this, Lacey vowed the bomber would never fly again. And it didn't.

Getting the B-17 to Oregon was one thing, but moving it another 15 miles to the Portland suburb of Milwaukie was something entirely different, and almost as impossible. Local officials denied Lacey permits to move the plane over the highway and streets. He even went to the Governor for help and was turned down.

Finally, with the aid of the power company and the police (who pretended not to notice) the bomber was taken apart and put on four flat-bed trucks in the middle of the night and hauled to its resting place in Milwaukie. There it was installed, 20 feet above the ground, a unique centerpiece over Lacey's gas station and restaurant.

For nearly half-a-century, the bomber, later named *Lacey's Lady,* was one of the biggest tourist attractions in Oregon. More than 1 million people climbed the steps to explore the inside to see what it would be like to sit in the cockpit of a famous WWII bomber. Newspapers and magazines everywhere wrote articles about *Lacey's Lady.* At one time, Art Lacey turned down a South American government's offer of $500,000 for the aircraft.

Down through the years, *Lacey's Lady* became a victim of weather, people taking things for keepsakes, and the inevitable vandalism. Lacey closed the gas station in 1990 and passed away in 2000.

The bomber still sits above the ground, but is no longer open to the public. With its nose missing, and its luster faded, the B-17 sits quietly above the bomber restaurant as a reminder of our victory over tyranny in World War II. Of course, to many, it's a monument to a spunky guy named Art Lacey who set his mind on doing the impossible to collect a $5.00 bet.

THE FURLOUGH

Donald Strand was a simple man. He worked the day shift at a tool plant in Chicago that paid him a modest wage, which he felt was sufficient to provide a decent living for his wife Dorothy and their young son Roger. He had been at the job for sixteen years, never interested in advancing himself and only content in taking what wage increase came about naturally. He walked twelve blocks to and from his work every day and boasted he missed only one day in all those years. That was when he sprained his ankle one morning stepping off the front porch on his way to work. He never owned a car and thought it was extravagant and unnecessary.

Raising young Roger was left entirely up to his wife, but when the boy needed discipline he felt it was his duty as the father to apply the punishment, which was most often very severe and without emotion. Roger would remember this as being about the only relationship he ever had with his father. There were never any father and son outings like camping trips or baseball games, despite the fact that Wrigley Field was within walking distance. The boy remembers going to a few movie matinees with his mother and one time to a company picnic that ended with his father getting drunk. Young Roger couldn't wait to graduate from high school and leave home. His mother never discouraged him.

Soon after Roger turned seventeen, his mother was struck by a delivery truck while crossing a street two blocks from their home. She was rushed to a hospital but died within hours because of head injuries. Roger was devastated. Following a simple funeral his father wrapped himself in total silence, leaving his son to mourn for his mother on his own. The two hardly spoke to each other. Now with his mother suddenly gone, Roger felt it was time to leave. He left a note for his father one morning, walked three blocks to catch a bus to a nearby suburb, and then stood in line at an Army recruiting office waiting for it to open. It was January, 1942, and the United States had been at war for over a month.

Donald Strand continued to walk every day to and from his job at the tool plant. It wasn't until five months after the death of his wife when a fellow worker asked how he and his son Roger were getting along that anybody knew the boy had joined the Army. That was all the information Donald gave. Nothing more, nothing less. Roger was in the Army. Period.

As the war years rolled ahead, Roger became involved in the Italian campaign where he was taken prisoner by the Germans just south of Rome. This lasted only two days when he and three other captured Americans escaped during a German retreat. He soon became a corporal and fought in several more combat battles until he was wounded in the leg by mortar fire. He was evacuated to an Army hospital in Rome, while back home his father was keeping much to himself at his job and only leaving his small house to buy food.

Then one day in early July, 1944, as Donald approached his house after a day's work, he noticed someone sitting on the steps leading to the front porch of his house. He couldn't make out who it was at first. Then as he got closer he saw it was a man in uniform. It was Roger. A sudden wave excitement came over him. A feeling he had never experienced before. As he reached the front steps, Roger stood up, steadying himself with a cane, and smiled as he said hello to his father. Donald stood silently for a moment, then made the final steps toward his son and embraced him. The two wept and held each other for what seemed like an eternity.

During the next hour Donald begged his son for forgiveness for the way he treated him as he was growing up. Roger forgave him and they hugged again as he explained to his father he had a train to catch and that he would soon be home for good because he was getting a medical discharge. They walked together to the bus stop, put their arms around each other once more, and soon Roger was on the bus and gone. The father stood there and watched the bus until it disappeared from view.

The next day at work Donald greeted his co-workers with a smile as he excitedly told them of his reunion with his son. Several commented they had never seen him so happy.

This abrupt change from a brooding, bitter old man to one with a cheerful and heartfelt compassion for others was almost more than they could accept. A miracle must have truly taken place. And Donald's warm and friendly personality never wavered until the day he died in 1953.

Roger received his medical discharge in August of 1944 and returned to Chicago to live with his father until late 1951. Their love for each other grew and his father couldn't stop asking his son for forgiveness. Roger finally told him to never bring it up again because all was truly forgiven. They even went to baseball games at Wrigley Field.

Roger finally married in 1951 when his father had to be committed to a nursing home. They continued to see each at least twice a week until Donald's death. Roger was told by the nursing staff that his father was a model patient and kind to everyone. He often told them about Roger's short furlough in 1944 and how, upon seeing him, his life changed forever and made him a new person. They said he would often weep when he told the story.

As Roger looks back over his father's sudden transformation that one day in 1944, he still wonders at the mystery of it all. He knew it was truly a miracle, because he could never bring himself to tell his father that he never came home that day on furlough. He was in an Army hospital in England.

THE SECRET WEAPON

What was the United State's greatest secret weapon in World War II? War historians will give you several answers, which would include, of course, the atom bomb. But when the war ended, and the years since have passed into half-a-century, certain classified records began to surface to reveal that our secret weapon was most likely a special contingent of Japanese-American volunteers.

According to Maj. Gen. Charles Willoughby, intelligence chief for General Douglas McArthur, their efforts saved over one million lives and shortened the war by two years.

Following the devastating blow at Pearl Harbor by the Japanese Empire, the United States quickly lost the Philippines. With our Pacific fleet almost destroyed at Pearl Harbor, it was feared the Japanese would now invade our western coastline. In two short months, our backs were suddenly against the wall.

But the Japanese commanders, in their arrogant confidence, didn't bother to put their wartime communications into code. After all, they figured their language looked and sounded too strange and complex for foreigners to decipher. And they certainly didn't figure on the 6,000 young Japanese-American men who volunteered from behind the barbed wire fences of their internment camps to serve as translators for the U.S. Army. If the Japanese warlords didn't know about them, neither did the American public. They were pledged to secrecy by the U.S. Government.

These Japanese-American linguists served in every major battle in the Pacific. They questioned captives, assuring them of humane treatment, which in turn brought about useful information. They eavesdropped on communications between Japanese pilots and their airfields, and read captured maps and orders to learn the Japanese troop strength and battle plans. From diaries and letters taken from dead soldiers they could detect the state of morale of the Japanese troops. Other captured documents indicated the enemy's problems of food and supply and the effect of our air attacks - all of such importance that on numerous occasions the information obtained caused a major shift in American plans of attack.

One captured Japanese soldier, who had been brainwashed by his superiors in believing that the Americans would torture and kill him, became convinced by his Japanese-American interrogator that he had nothing to fear. In turn, the prisoner, a former shipyard worker, drew detailed sketches of every type of ship in Japan's navy.

Another incredible piece of information they picked up had a direct effect on the Allied D-Day landings halfway around the world. It occurred when the Japanese ambassador to Berlin was given an extensive tour of Germany's defenses along the English Channel. The excited ambassador promptly sent a detailed description to Tokyo. His message was intercepted in Turkey and sent to Virginia, where the Japanese-American linguists translated it. The details were then sent to General Dwight D. Eisenhower.

All told, the Japanese-Americans translated 20 million captured documents and questioned over 14,000 prisoners. They also served with Allied forces from Great Britain, Canada, Australia, New Zealand, India and China. General Douglas McArthur underscored their part in winning the war when he said, "Never in military history did an army know so much about the enemy prior to an actual engagement."

The United States government kept this vital war contribution by Japanese-Americans under wraps for more than 50 years. Only recently has their extraordinary service and patriotism come to light.

What the Axis countries of Germany and Japan failed to comprehend during WWII was that the United States, unlike themselves, was not a nation made up of one single nationality, but one comprised of all races and religions that would bond together when their freedom was threatened. The enemy's indifference to this fact eventually brought them down in defeat; an historical fact that today's foreign nations supporting terrorism should study very carefully. If anyone doubts that the American public no longer has the resolve to react in the same manner as their grandparents did following Pearl Harbor should remember September 11th. The American reaction to that cowardly attack was just a glimpse of what they are still capable and willing to sacrifice in rising together again, despite mixed nationalities, to defend and safeguard their democracy.

NOW YOU SEE IT, NOW YOU DON'T!

One of the most bizarre incidents to come out of World War II was a secret navy wartime project so unusual and incredible that even die-hard science fiction buffs are finding hard to believe.

Despite denials by the Office of Naval Information that the incident ever actually happened, there has been over the past nearly 50 years a persistent and revealing investigative program undertaken by certain scientists and researchers who now claim, much to their growing astonishment, that this impossible experiment did in fact take place.

It was known as The Philadelphia Experiment.

In 1943, the navy destroyer escort *U.S.S. Eldridge*, according to uncovered secret documents, simply vanished into thin air in the Philadelphia shipyard. Moments later it reappeared in Norfolk, Virginia and then reappeared back in Philadelphia. Those researching the incident claim this sleight of hand was caused by a series of planned magnetic manifestations. Meaning, some scientists figured out how to cause a shift in the molecular composition of matter, induced by intensified and resonant magnetism which could cause an object to vanish. Got that? Remember, we're talking nearly 60 years ago when this heady stuff was reserved strictly for the comic pages and movie serials.

During the course of the investigation, some of the navy personnel who were on board the ship at the time reluctantly came forward and gave detailed accounts of suffering severe psychological after-effects from the incident. Some experienced double vision, hallucinations and painful fainting spells. And there were claims that several had died. According to the survivors, they were discharged as mentally unfit, told to keep a lid on it, and if they were ever questioned about the incident the navy could brush it off as something cooked up by a bunch of loonies.

Unlike the *U.S.S. Eldridge*, interest in the Philadelphia Experiment just wouldn't disappear. At first, this intriguing story was looked upon by certain writers and members of the scientific community with an attitude of amused curiosity. Then it gradually grew into a serious obsession as they began to uncover various conveniently missing documents and more witnesses. They even located a few key scientists who appeared to have inside knowledge about the experiment and who had been mysteriously restricted to living quietly in isolated areas.

It's a known fact that the United States during World War II was engaged in three projects that came under the umbrella of science fiction. One was concerned with antigravity, the second one with invisibility, and the third one with the atom bomb.

When the success of the atom bomb ended the war almost overnight in 1945, work on the other two projects was suspended.

But if they were successful in making a destroyer escort and its crew vanish into thin air back in 1943, almost two years before the atom bomb was dropped, why then wasn't this project of invisibility developed first into the weapon to end the war? The answer, the researchers claim, lies in the fact that the effect the experiment had on the crew turned out to be more devastating than the planners had anticipated. So it was stopped.

Among the interesting revelations to come out of the investigation into the Philadelphia Experiment was that Albert Einstein was employed by the navy during those years of the experiment. Was he involved in the project? Nobody is talking and his work is still classified as top secret.

It boggles the mind to think that over half-a-century ago we might have successfully unlocked the cosmic secrets of matter, space and time. Something we all know was right up Einstein's alley.

RAH! RAH! REICHSMARSCHALL

Probably one of the most peculiar, and certainly eccentric, persons in the Nazi regime was Hermann Goering.

One of the very first members of that infamous party, he was one of Hitler's closest confidants from the very beginning when he was injured in the 1923 Beer Hall Putsch in Munich. Why the German dictator kept him around and put him in charge of important offices was a mystery even to some of the higher Nazis officials. Behind closed doors he was looked upon as a joke. And he had a passion for a certain wardrobe item that will probably leave its mark on Germany until the end of time.

Goering was a fighter pilot during World War I and was credited in shooting down twenty-two British and French aircraft. He became a German war hero and was hailed as one of Germany's finest. This was potent stuff for a pilot who was already known to his comrades as "Struttin' Herman." When Manfred von Richtofen, the legendary Red Baron, was shot down and killed, Goering was put in charge of the famous fighter pilot's squadron. Germany eventually lost the war, but Goering went home as a revered war ace.

With Hitler's rise to power from the mid-1920s to the 1930s, Goering was goose stepping right behind him. When the Nazis took over complete control of Germany, he talked Hitler into letting him be Commander in Chief of the German Air Force, the Prime Minister of Prussia, the President of the Reichstag, the head of the Gestapo, and Supreme Head of the National

Weather Bureau. He was also named *Reichsmarschall* of numerous other government departments, and he had a spiffy uniform tailor-made for each position. In fact, he was nicknamed the "Flying Tailor."

He had a passion for dressing up in these special, and often garish, uniforms. He had become so into himself that he felt he was adding a luster to his appearance by applying rouge to his cheeks and painting his toenails. He often smelled as though he had just taken a bath in a tub full of Bay Rum. Add his addiction to drugs, such as morphine, and you had a wild and crazy guy. There weren't many, to say the least, who wanted to stand near him during social functions or official gatherings. His outlandish appearance was the talk of the party's inner circle, and it was said that even Hitler was a little concerned, and sometimes amused, about where this was all taking his overweight *Reichsmarschall*.

It was in the early 1930s when Goering hit the summit for indulgence in flashy uniforms when he noticed a picture of a coat in an American magazine. What he saw, as the story goes, was a Yale cheerleader decked out in a full-length raccoon coat doing his rah-rah thing with a large megaphone. To Goering this coat was pure euphoria. But it did present a problem since there were no raccoons to be found anywhere in Germany.

Goering first instructed an aide to contact an American coat manufacturer to outfit him with a raccoon coat, but there were none in stock big enough to fit his three hundred pound frame. They would, however, be more than happy to make one to his specifications. Goering turned them down because he had a better idea. An ingenious one at that. He would make his own raccoon coat, maybe not just one but several. Perhaps enough to outfit all the top ranking Nazi officials.

After much preparation, Goering was able to import four raccoons from the United States. There was no problem getting them through German customs because he was in charge of that too. He immediately started a breeding program that would soon have little raccoons running about everywhere. He would gaze into the future and see his "project raccoon" blossoming into a major industry within the German fashion world. He would be the envy of the Nazi party.

But the raccoons didn't breed on the scale Goering had hoped they would. They did their thing when they wanted to and often would escape their pens and scratch their keepers.

After a period of time Goering became frustrated when the little varmints hadn't even reproduced enough for a coat collar. His raccoon coat empire was crumbling. Was it because the little rascals were Americans? In any event, the pompous Nazi official ordered the doors closed on his great experiment and the raccoons done away with — like release them in a German forest somewhere. Just get rid of them. Nazi officials were snickering behind his back already.

Maybe Goering should have done what the Nazis usually did in those cases. Exterminate them. Leave no traces. Instead, his subordinates followed his orders and released what raccoons there were deep in a forest. Goering's great raccoon coat empire was a fizzle, and now they were gone and forgotten forever as far as Goering was concerned. At least that's what he thought.

As the time passed through the war years, and the Nazi domination over Europe was finally destroyed, our little, furry American imports literally took over the German forests, multiplying at such an incredible rate it would have brought a smile to Goering's face. (Who, by the way, committed suicide before he was to be hanged as a result of the Nuremberg war trials in 1946.)

To this day, all of Europe is infested with an out-of-control population of raccoons that has reached monstrous proportions. They are everywhere, even in the cities. Thanks to *Reichsmarschall* Hermann Goering and a Yale cheerleader.

THE MAGNIFIED HERO

When the Japanese Empire struck Pearl Harbor on December 7, 1941, the blow was more devastating than the America public was lead to believe at the time. As destructive as it was, the government was able to cover up most of the staggering facts caused by the surprise attack.

The government feared that if the public knew our entire Pacific fleet had been practically destroyed, hundreds of aircraft wiped out, and over 3,000 people killed, a state of panic might set in. And it didn't help matters any when the Japanese immediately invaded the Philippines and started sweeping through Southeast Asia. The United States had been blind-sided and the dark clouds of war began rolling swiftly over the Pacific.

Despite efforts to suppress as much of the bad news as possible, a wave of impending doom, nevertheless, began to settle over the American people. Both the Hawaiian Islands and the West Coast of the United States braced for a Japanese invasion. Many military officials believed it was sure to come before Christmas. Our defenses didn't exist. The American people needed something desperately to lift their spirits and get them back up on their feet. They needed a hero fast — even if someone had to create one. And that's what the military did in just three days following Pearl Harbor.

On December 10, 1941, the Japanese were wasting little time rushing troops ashore in the Philippines and over-running poorly equipped American and Philippine forces. A small contingent of American B-17 bombers began attacking Japanese shipping and landing crafts. One B-17 in particular, piloted by U.S. Army Air Force Captain Colin P. Kelly, Jr., missed its target and was starting the return flight when it was attacked by one of Japan's ace pilots, Saburo Sakai.

As the bomber became engulfed in flames, those who survived the incident said Kelly held the plane as level as he could so that his crew could bail out. Kelly, however, couldn't get himself out, and as a result died in the crash. He would be the first West Point graduate to be killed in World War II and his plane the first B-17 lost in combat.

Hero, indeed. But someone in the U.S. high command felt Kelly's ordeal needed a little more seasoning. Thus, the legend of Colin P. Kelly, Jr. was created, and America had its first major war hero.

The first change in the story, from what really happened, was that Kelly's bombing run was announced as a success and that he did hit his intended target. They did stay with the facts, however, about him being attacked on his return flight and that he steadied his aircraft so that his crew could bail out. At this point, adding more drama to the situation must have been irresistible.

Instead of sticking with the true story about Kelly going down in flames, they had him deliberately slamming his doomed bomber into the big Japanese battleship *Haruna*, which was lying just off Philippine coast. Newspaper headlines and radio commentators brought Kelly's heroics to the American public. As a teenager, I can remember listening to Eddie Cantor devoting the last minutes of his weekly radio program to Kelly's great sacrifice. Flags were displayed on porches and buildings. This was the kind of hero we needed to rally around during those first uncertain days of the war: the kind of stuff that sold millions of dollars in war bonds.

Actually, the *Haruna* was the last surviving Japanese battleship of the war, finally sinking from an American air attack in Kure Harbor on July 28, 1945. Myth also had Kelly being awarded the Congressional Medal of Honor. The truth is he received a posthumous Distinguished Service Cross.

Interestingly, President Franklin D. Roosevelt wrote a letter that was to be opened by whoever was President in 1956 to appoint Colin Kelly III to West Point. Little did he realize that the future President would be his top general during WWII, Dwight D. Eisenhower. Young Kelly grew up and went to West Point and served as a chaplain with the rank of major.

In looking back, the true story about Colin P. Kelly, Jr. would have been more than enough to make him an American hero. How could we not have accepted his sacrifice with patriotic pride when he stayed with his burning aircraft so that his crew could bail out?

Really, they don't come anymore heroic than that.

THE BIG COVER-UP

On the evening of December 2, 1943, the citizens of Bari, Italy were beginning to relax from the weariness of war now that the liberating Allied armies had pushed the Germans out of their city and far into the northern part of the country. They were able to gather more freely in the seaport's narrow streets and take leisurely strolls along the picturesque sea wall. Near the center of the city two American servicemen baseball teams were playing to a capacity crowd. On this particular evening the war was a long way away.

The Allied forces had established Bari as a major supply port for their advancing armies. In the crowded harbor, more than fifty ships were waiting to unload cargo that would be vital in the final assault to drive the Germans out of Italy. There were so many ships that they almost touched each other.

What was about to happen at that moment would result in one of the most devastating disasters of World War II; a nightmare that would be a prelude of the horror that would continue to this day. Yet only a few people, even more than half-a-century later, would ever hear of the Bari incident. It would become the biggest cover-up of World War II.

As the war zone moved further away from Bari, the protection of its harbor was left up to the British whose defense system had become extremely loose, to say the least. The concern of the Allied ships was to get their cargo unloaded as quickly as possible while mine sweepers swept the entrance to the harbor for mines left behind by the Germans. Things were moving at a snail's pace, especially for one nervous captain of a particular American Liberty Ship.

At preciously 7:30 p.m., a low droning sound was heard approaching the city from somewhere to the north. As it grew louder, a few looked skyward and detected nothing. Then suddenly, from out of nowhere, the German Luftwaffe swooped down low over the harbor. Ships began exploding almost in unison. The concussion literally knocked down buildings and set fire to people in the streets. Docks were destroyed instantly as the harbor became a flaming inferno. The explosion from one vessel loaded with munitions was so horrific it sent a giant tidal wave over the pier and into the streets. In twenty minutes it was all over.

A total of seventeen ships were sunk. Four of those were completely obliterated. Eight more were seriously damaged and the town of Bari lay in ruins. It would become the worst bombing of Allied shipping since Pearl Harbor, leaving more than 1,000 Allied servicemen and more than 1,000 civilians killed.

Why was there no advance warning of the attack? Why were the U.S. Navy Armed Guard gunners aboard most of the ships ordered by the British not to fire back at the German aircraft? And why would there be countless survivors of the raid who would mysteriously die over the next half-century because of the bombing?

Answers to the first two questions could only be due to the lack of a proper British harbor defense and an inadequate communication system with the ships in the harbor. As for the answer to the last question, it lay below deck in the cargo hold of the American Liberty Ship *S.S. John Harvey.*

This woman survived one of the biggest enemy bombing disasters of WWII that is still affecting people today. Why did the allies, especially the United States, try to cover it up and Winston Churchill denied it happened?

The ship was secretly carrying mustard poison gas — a direct violation of the Geneva Gas Protocol of 1925. Although the United States did not sign the protocol, it did agree to abide by it. The use of chemical warfare was outlawed after its use in the First World War, but there was evidence in this war that Nazi Germany was stockpiling poison gas. President Roosevelt opposed the use of chemical weapons, but knew we had to be prepared in case the enemy used them. With the Germans in retreat from Italy, and the D-Day landings not far off, there was fear that Hitler would go to his stockpile of poison gas as a last resort to defend his borders.

The *S.S. John Harvey's* lethal cargo was shipped from the United States to Bari, Italy under complete secrecy. The captain didn't even know he was carrying it until he opened his special orders upon arrival at the Italian port. His persistence about getting the poison gas immediately off his ship, and properly stored by the

U.S. Army in accordance to his orders, was met with little concern from port officials who were kept in the dark about the deadly cargo. Then it was too late. The surprise air strike scored a direct hit on the *Harvey* and all hands were lost.

The total number of deaths caused by the raid was estimated to be more than two thousand and a city of 200,000 was reduced to rubble. The actual number of deaths, however, may never be known. Thousands of survivors of the bombing, civilians and Allied personnel alike, would die over the next half century due to the toxic contamination — a fact that the leaders of the Allied nations, especially the United States and Great Britain, would deny for over fifty years as the cause of the deaths, let alone admit that the poison gas was even on the ship. After all, nobody could prove it was since the *Harvey* blew apart.

The problem was that a dark toxic haze hung over the port and wouldn't go away. In the harbor, a steady leakage of chemicals kept seeping to the surface from the sunken wreckage of the *Harvey.* Those who were there, and who for years would suffer the appalling after-effects of the raid, knew very well about the hell that took place there on December 2, 1943.

Only recently have all the facts about the Bari nightmare come to light. British Prime Minister Winston Churchill, in particular, emphatically denied that any mustard poison gas was present on the *S.S. John Harvey* that day in Bari. He would take that denial to his grave in 1965.

A TEAM EFFORT

On Sunday morning, December 7, 1941, I was coming down the steps of the United Presbyterian church in Albany, Oregon with a group of high school boys when I overheard a friend of mine sitting on his parked bicycle tell someone that the Japanese had just bombed Pearl Harbor. One of our group said, "Where's Pearl Harbor?" Another said, "I think it's in Alaska." And I remember thinking to myself, "Why would anybody want to bomb Alaska?"

Any of us who are old enough can remember exactly where we were and what we were doing when we heard the news. I can vividly recall going home after church and seeing my dad and mom sitting in the kitchen listening to the radio. I couldn't grasp yet what all this meant. War in Europe had been so far away and now we were in it. I had just turned fifteen and I can recall my mom saying they wouldn't take me because I was too young and the war would be over before I would have to go. I would eventually become of age, enlist in the navy and serve in the South Pacific.

As I sat at the kitchen table, I turned away from the war talk and directed my attention to the more important things concerning a young teenage boy: the *Oregonian* sports page and the football scores from the day before.

Across the top of the page a headline blared: "Texas 71 Oregon 7." I shuddered. At least my favorite team, the Oregon State Beavers, had ended their season the week before and was going to the Rose Bowl. Years later, I would think about how the attack on Pearl Harbor did the Oregon Duck fans a favor. The result of the Texas game was quickly shoved back into the dark corners of the minds of most Oregon fans, and mercifully forgotten even to this day.

But what caught my interest that day, which I never forgot, was the story on the second page about Hawaii defeating Willamette 20-6 in Honolulu. What a neat trip, I thought, for the Willamette team. At the time I remember wondering if they were okay and would they be able to get back home.

What did happen to them is something very few people know about even to this day.

Early that Sunday morning, the Willamette University team and a contingent of fans from Salem, Oregon, stood in front of the Moana Hotel waiting for a tour bus to take them to Pearl Harbor. Suddenly, they noticed large, dark clouds rising in the distance that quickly filled the air with heavy, oily smoke. They knew something devastating was taking place, but it would be some time later before they would get word that Pearl Harbor had been bombed by Japanese aircraft

In the confusion that followed the attack, the football team and their supporters stayed close to their hotel pondering what all this meant. What was to happen to them? Then the team knew what they had to do. Worrying about how they were going to get home was now a secondary concern.

The team immediately volunteered their services to the army to do what they could to help fend off a possible follow-up invasion by the Japanese. They strung barbed wire along Waikiki

Beach at low tide, dug trenches, and were issued World War I bolt-action Springfield rifles. After a brief training session on how to handle the rifles, they were given orders to defend the beach. Others were sent into the hills above Honolulu to protect the water towers and storage tanks. They moved from the Moana Hotel into a high school dormitory and went on day and night sentry rotation.

Twelve days later on December 19th, the team and their fans finally left Hawaii aboard the *S.S. President Calvin Coolidge*, a luxury liner that had arrived in Hawaii with evacuees from the Philippines. The ship now added the gravely wounded servicemen from the attack. During the seven-day voyage back to the states, members of the Willamette team and their followers, which included future Oregon Governor Douglas McKay, assisted with the wounded on day and night shifts. They landed safely in San Francisco on Christmas Day. It would be the last time they would all see each other.

Almost every player from that football team enlisted in the military service. Only one of them would not survive the war. They went on to careers as teachers, lawyers and business people. One became a federal judge.

The 1941 Willamette football team would later be inducted into the Willamette University Athletic Hall of Fame to honor its 8-2 record and for being the second leading scoring team in the nation.

But more specifically, it was to honor them for their extra service to the nation in a time of crisis.

THE MISUNDERSTOOD LOOK

World War II produced several memorable photographs that gave testimony to the great struggle and sacrifice the Allied nations endured to save freedom. Probably two of the most famous are the flag raising on Iwo Jima and General Douglas McArthur wading ashore in the Philippines.

The one photo that I remember most, however, was one of British Prime Minister Winston Churchill. It appeared on the cover of *Life* magazine shortly after Pearl Harbor. You know the one. Standing straight-backed in a black suit and bow tie, one hand on his hip and the other gripping the back of a chair, his eyes blazed straight ahead and his jaw clenched in defiance, he stood as if warning the Nazis that they would never, ever defeat England.

Up to this point, the British had been fighting the war for more than two years and mostly on the defensive. The photo became an instant morale booster for all Englishmen and a badly needed inspiration to the people of the United States who had just been blind-sided by the Japanese.

But Churchill's classic look of determination in standing his ground against tyranny was not what the Prime Minister was expressing. He was actually expressing a desire to strangle the photographer.

It all started in late December, 1941, when the Canadian Prime Minister, McKenzie King, contacted a young Turkish immigrant in Canada by the name of Yousuf Karsh, an excellent but little-known photographer. King informed Karsh that Churchill, who had flown to the United States, would soon be in Canada to address both houses of Parliament and he was being commissioned to take Churchill's portrait. For the young photographer it was the assignment of a lifetime.

Churchill addressed Parliament, and then was led into a small room for his portrait.

It immediately became apparent that someone had failed to inform the Prime Minister of what was about to take place. He became furious, and nervously paced about the room chewing on his ever-present cigar. When Karsh was ready, he ushered Churchill to a position next to a chair and held out an ash tray for him. The Prime Minister silently refused it as he glared at the photographer.

Just about the time Karsh was ready to click the shutter, he suddenly stopped. At this moment in time the young photographer said three bold words, and then made a daring move that would create one of the greatest photo-portraits of all time.

"Forgive me, sir," Karsh said. He then stepped forward and removed Churchill's cigar from his mouth.

Churchill was stunned into silence. He bristled with anger, but said not a word as Karsh quickly squeezed the shutter release. His hostile reaction to not being notified about the photo-shoot, and to Karsh in particular, was captured on film forever, mistakenly accepted by the Allied nations as a heroic expression of defiance toward the enemy.

The legendary portrait that expressed defiance against the tyranny of Nazi Germany and the steadfast courage of the British. Actually, it meant something entirely different.

Within weeks this remarkable photo would appear in newspapers and magazines throughout the free world. It is still the most used portrait of Churchill.

As for Yousuf Karsh, the photo made him internationally famous. For many years, even long after the war had ended, he became much in demand to photograph the world's greatest leaders.

And Churchill, not long afterwards, wrote Karsh and congratulated him on what was to become the Prime Minister's personal favorite of all the photos ever taken of him.

THE MARK 3

Following the Battle of Midway in May of 1942, the tide of the war in the Pacific gradually started swinging around in the favor of the United States. The Japanese domination in that part of the world, up until that famous sea battle, was overwhelming. If the Japanese were to be defeated it would most surely have to be one island at a time, starting in the south Pacific and working north to the very shores of Japan. Most of those in the American military high command figured it would take anywhere from five to ten years to accomplish the feat. And it would cost nearly half-a-million American lives.

But the U.S. military masterminds in the Pacific came up with an ingenious plan. Instead of taking one island at a time, why not take one strategic island, skip maybe one or two, and then capture another island. This way the United States could blockade the skipped islands, thus stranding thousands of Japanese soldiers and airplanes by literally isolating them, and then move more quickly up the ladder to retaking the Philippines. The battle plan was adopted and eventually the Pacific was retaken from the Japanese. By July, 1945, U.S. forces stood ready at the very doorstep of Japan, ready for the final onslaught that would end the war.

At the beginning of this plan, which started with the capture of Guadalcanal, the Japanese high command in Tokyo was desperately working on a secret weapon that would surely halt any further American advancement. Their intelligence ring hinted to them that something mysterious was also being developed in the United States as a secret weapon, but they couldn't quite get a handle on it. If it was to be used on their troops they wanted to get their weapon perfected first to defeat the Americans.

The Japanese secret weapon had the code name Mark 3. It was a huge shell casing that could only be fired from a battleship. Inside this shell, which weighed over one ton, was enough room to pack in more than 300 artillery shells. The plan was to fire this cumbersome monstrosity well over 100,000 feet in the air and then have it explode, which in turn would release the more than 300 artillery shells and send them to earth raining over an entire American military formation. The result would be awesome. One shot could wipe out a whole division. The designers were ordered to proceed immediately on the Mark 3.

On paper the Mark 3 looked menacing. But getting it up off the drawing board was quite something else. The construction of the big shell, which some say was made from American scrap metal brought from the U.S.A in the late 1930s, took months to complete. Then came the careful placing inside the casing of the more than 300 artillery shells. A special crane was devised to hoist the big bomb on board the battleship *Mutsu*. The Japanese high command was so certain of its eventual success that they ordered another Mark 3 to be taken aboard the battleship. You know the old saying, "If one is good, two is that much better." So it seemed.

As the war raged in the Pacific, the American plan of island hopping was slowly taking its toll on the Japanese military. Now was the time the Japanese needed to activate their secret weapon, the Mark 3. In early June of 1943, the *Mutsu* set sail for an undisclosed battle zone in the South Pacific with the two lethal weapons on board. The big battle wagon was steaming through the Inland Sea just southwest of Japan when suddenly it blew sky high. Debris and bodies were blown and scattered over miles of ocean. Very few would survive the disaster. The destruction and loss of lives was one of the worst in Japanese naval history.

What really happened aboard the *Mutsu* has never been officially revealed, but the few Japanese sailors who did survive the explosion, and eventually the war, all pointed to the two big mysterious bombs aboard ship. Some said it happened when one of the Mark 3s came unsecured and bumped into something setting it off. Others claimed it was caused by a sailor who accidentally detonated it while setting some sort of timer. It's hard to believe, however, that anybody who made it through that catastrophe would actually know what really happened aboard the *Mutsu*.

Further construction of the Mark 3, which was to swing the balance of the war in favor of the Japanese, was suspended because of the danger involved in handling the big bomb. And it's ironic to think that some American discarded scrap metal, like a housewife's old frying pan, a kid's metal red wagon, or parts from an old Model A Ford, would play a major role in destroying Japan's secret weapon before it could be used on American troops.

THE REAL ALL-AMERICANS

At the close of every college football season, one of the great American gridiron pastimes among newspaper and magazine sportswriters is selecting the season's number-one All-America football team.

As a youngster, I remember laying on the living room floor and writing out my own selection and giving it to my dad, who in turn would take it to the office and show his co-workers. They applauded my selections, I'm told. But then I guess they had to. My Dad was the boss.

Back in those days, more than sixty years ago, it was sort of a fad for everyone, including kids and barber shop experts, to do their own All-America team. Of course, then it was only one team which consisted of eleven men. Today, they list twenty-two because they have both offensive and defensive teams. It was more fun selecting them the old way.

I then got to talking with an old friend of mine, a former sportswriter, about who we thought were the greatest eleven college players who would make up the all-time All-America team. We tossed names around from our era such as Tommy Harmon, Johnny Lujack, Bronco Nagurski and Leon Hart. We quickly realized that if you had to select eleven specific players you would never completely agree on the same names.

This got us to thinking. If you had to pick one particular college football team that would best represent the greatest All-America team ever, which would it be? One of Notre Dame's many fine teams? How about Army when they had Blanchard and Davis? There are also a number of USC teams to pick from during the glory days of the thirties. And of course, you would have to consider some of the great teams that came out of Nebraska, Ohio State and Michigan. And don't forget Alabama.

We decided that when you get right down to it, there was really only one true All-America college football team: the 1940-41 Montana State College Bobcats.

Let's stop here for a moment. If you're expecting to read about a team that stream-rolled every opponent then you're in for a surprise. During those two seasons they won only five games, lost eight and tied two. In one game they lost 54-0 to the Drake Bulldogs and had only fifteen men in uniform — hardly a record worthy of an All-America status.

The fact that Montana State could even put eleven men on the field at one time was almost a miracle in its self. The school's requirement for all male students to be in the ROTC was taking a heavy toll on the football roster as the nation started building for war. What the Bobcats achieved on the gridiron, however, was not what made this team of eleven young men special.

When Pearl Harbor was struck on December 7, 1941, the nation went into high gear in mobilizing for the war. Millions of young men went into uniform for the long uphill struggle to save freedom. The entire starting eleven for Montana State heard the call to arms and were in the military by early 1942.

When the war was over, more than 400,000 young men had given their lives. Counted amongst that awesome death total was every one of those eleven football players from Montana State College. Truly, the real All-America team.

GINA

In May, 1943, following a raid on Italian military positions in Sardinia, an American pilot in a P-38 began to run out of fuel in his attempt to return to his base in North Africa. His only choice was to land his aircraft somewhere on the enemy island and make his escape into the hills. With little effort, he set the plane down safely in a field, but was immediately surrounded by Italian soldiers and taken away.

The capture of this unusual looking American fighter plane with its unique twin fuselage intrigued the Italian military officials. Especially Guido Rossi, Italy's top fighter ace. He had an idea to put the American P-38 to work for the Italian Air Force as an American fighter plane just the way it was - stars and all. He approached Mussolini with his plan, and the Italian dictator enthusiastically approved.

Rossi took over the captured P-38 and set out on his calculated missions. He would fly the skies alone in search of straggling American bombers on their return flights to North Africa. His preference was the unsuspecting crippled bombers trying to make it safely back alone. His strategy was to fly alongside the bomber and offer to fly protection for them. Then when the bomber's crew relaxed, Rossi would fall behind and open fire, shooting them down. The Italian ace scored more than a dozen kills and managed to go undetected.

Then in late June, Rossi was again on the prowl when he encountered a lone B-17 attempting to make it back to North Africa with two engines gone — another sitting duck. As usual, he radioed the American bomber pilot he would be glad to escort them back to the base. After a few minutes had elapsed, he dropped back and opened fire. The B-17 burst into flames and crashed killing the entire crew, except for the pilot, U.S. Air Force first lieutenant Harold Fisher, who eventually found his way safely back to his base.

Being the only person to ever survive one of Rossi's sneak attacks, Fisher vowed revenge. Intelligence told him that the famous Italian flying ace had a hot temper and a beautiful and vivacious wife by the name of Gina. He also found out she was behind Allied lines in an Italian village that had been captured by the Americans. Armed with this information, Fisher had a plan he knew would bring down the disguised Italian.

With his commanding officer's permission, Fisher took another B-17 bomber and had it outfitted with special armor and extra firepower. Then he had Gina's picture and name painted on each side of the B-17. The trap was set, and it was time to go hunting.

The decoy B-17 took to the skies alone, with Fisher as its pilot, and headed for the air-route normally taken by the returning American bombers. As expected, it wasn't long until Rossi appeared with his P-38. As he pulled alongside the B-17 to tell them by radio he would protect them back to their base, he gasped as he saw his wife's picture and name sprawled across the nose of the bomber. In a futile attempt to hide his anger, Rossi wanted to know what this was all about.

"It's in honor of my new Italian girlfriend," replied Fisher, as though he was talking to a fellow American pilot. "She's an incredible woman to live with."

This infuriated Rossi so much that he quickly abandoned his normal rear attack and recklessly circled around for a head-on assault. Just what Fisher would hope he would do, and the gunners on the decoy B-17 were ready. Rossi had hardly maneuvered his captured P-38 into position for the attack when he was blasted from the sky. The charade was over.

Guido Rossi was picked up by an Allied air-sea rescue and spent the rest of the war as a prisoner. Harold Fisher was awarded the Distinguished Flying Cross and his crew each received an Air Medal. Fisher was later killed in 1948 during the Berlin air lift.

The Italian pilot's wife Gina was never heard from again. If she's still alive, she no doubt is unaware of her important role in helping to bring down her back-stabbing husband and his captured P-38.

As for Rossi, if he did survive the war, and with his temper, you can bet he probably tracked Gina down somewhere and made her pay the price for "cheating" on him with an American B-17 pilot.

THE MYSTERY OF THE PE-56

It was shortly after noon on April 23, 1945, when the U.S. Navy Sub Chaser PE-56, during a routine patrol only five miles off the coast of Maine, exploded from a direct hit by a torpedo. Within minutes, the World War I vintage vessel sank in the icy Atlantic, taking with her almost the entire crew. It would be the greatest loss of U.S. Navy personal in New England waters during World War II.

A few survivors made it to the coast near Cape Elizabeth, but their story of the enemy submarine attack was met with a puzzling response from navy officials. Despite some of the survivor's account that a submarine conning tower was sighted following the attack, the navy attributed the incident to a boiler explosion. The officials refused to review any further information concerning the sinking and Purple Hearts were denied to the surviving crew and to those who were killed.

For fifty-six years, the navy stood firm on its decision about what happened to the PE-56, but not the few survivors and family members of those who perished in the explosion. Among those was John Mickelsen, whose father was a chief machinist mate aboard the ill fated ship. He and the others persisted in their quest to have the truth be known.

Through their relentless investigations, they discovered from German records that in early 1945, the U-Boat U-853 had been patrolling the waters off Maine about the time of the incident. But there was no solid proof that the German submarine actually sank the sub chaser. Something more was going to be needed other than the survivor's testimonials to make their case stick: concrete evidence in the way of a written record that the U.S. Navy knew that the Germans had actually torpedoed the ship. Nothing to their knowledge existed, and with the passing of so much time it was beginning to look hopeless. Then along came Paul Lawton.

Lawton was a New England attorney and underwater archeologist who became intrigued with the story as it was related to him by Paul Westerlund, whose father had been a victim of the sinking. Lawton's interest in the matter was just the right ingredient to energize the project. He had inside connections and a bulldog determination that could usually open a door somewhere. He enlisted the aid of Congressman Moakey, but the navy refused to see them. Case closed. But Lawton didn't back down.

Then, after long hours of hard work, the New England attorney suddenly hit on something extraordinary. He located the woman who had actually transcribed the original board of inquiry session back in 1945. More amazing was that the woman still had her steno pads of the meeting. Lawton was stunned when he saw them. This is what they had been looking for.

This time Lawton and Moakey went back to the naval authorities loaded for bear and ready with the facts. The Congressman requested that the navy once again hand over the complete records of the incident. He was told emphatically they didn't exist.

"Then perhaps you would like a copy" Moakey replied. "You will find the complete transcript in this folder."

For the first time in U.S. Naval history, the manner in which an American warship was sunk was reversed. On June 8, 2002, aboard the *USS Salem* in Boston Harbor, Purple Hearts were finally awarded to the remaining three crew members and to families of those who were killed in the attack or had passed on during the ensuing years. The navy had finally admitted the PE-56 Sub Chaser had been torpedoed by a German submarine.

But there is still a cloud of mystery hovering over the incident. Why was one seaman ordered to lie about what happened that day in his letters to family members of the crew?

Why was another crew member not given a Purple Heart despite the fact he spent 14 days in a hospital because of his injuries? Why did no one from the navy or administration attend the Purple Heart ceremony aboard the USS Salem?

The big mystery, of course, is why was there a cover-up? The transcript of the inquiry never gave a clue.

MORE THAN A PRETTY FACE

Ever since I was about eight years old I've been a movie buff. Especially about the movies made from the early 1930s through the 1950s. I went to them constantly and read every book I could on Hollywood. I don't go to movies much now, but I'll tune in to an old flick whenever I can on television. My main interest in them was trying to figure out how they shot a particular scene, or catching cutaway mistakes. This was usually done much to the annoyance of anyone sitting next to me who was trying to enjoy the movie the way you are suppose to.

I also could name hundreds of movie stars and character actors. When World War II broke out, I found it interesting to see which ones went into the military and what they did. Which brings me to an actor named Sterling Hayden. There are many from my generation, I'm sure, who remember him. He was the blonde heart-throb opposite Madeline Carroll (remember her?) in *Hurricane* in 1940. He couldn't act, but the young girls didn't care. He made a couple of other forgettable movies in there somewhere, and then came Pearl Harbor.

With so many movie actors enlisting, the fan magazines had a field day writing about each one and what heroes they were all going to be. All except one: Sterling Hayden. He did enlist, but what was said about him didn't appear in a fan magazine but in a movie critic's column. It was something to the effect that he was too pretty, his on-screen machismo was phony to the point of being laughable, and that this critic couldn't see him being heroic and charging the enemy head on. Ouch! I remembered that article, and got to thinking not too long ago that I should, out of curiosity, do a little research on Mr. Hayden's military record.

Hayden was recruited for some unknown reason by OSS chief "Wild Bill" Donovan for commando and parachute training. It was during one of the parachute practice jumps in England that the actor broke his ankle, tore up his knee and injured his spine. Following his recovery, he went back to the states, tested PT boats in New York Harbor and then was selected for Marine officer training. After receiving his commission, he rejoined the OSS and later shipped off to Monopoli, Italy where he was put in command of a group that smuggled arms and equipment across the Adriatic Sea to Yugoslavian partisans. Hayden had under his command more than four hundred guerrillas and twenty two boats.

And he wasn't content to sit back in Italy.

On several occasions, Hayden himself made the dangerous trip behind German lines, putting his life on the line as he fought alongside his Yugoslavian comrades. More than once, he narrowly escaped from being caught or killed. When the war ended he was discharged as a Marine captain.

But Hayden apparently took his "comrade" fellowship a little too seriously when he was hanging out with Tito and his partisan fighters. He had joined the communist party and before long was called on the carpet before the House Un-American Activities Committee. He came to his senses, as he put it, and renounced his membership.

Hayden resumed his acting career after the war with parts in *Suddenly* opposite Frank Sinatra, and in *The Asphalt Jungle* with

Marilyn Monroe. One of his most important and memorable roles was that of the chief of police on the take in *The Godfather*.

Overall, Sterling Hayden may not have been much of an actor, but he was sure one heck of a fighting Marine who took his fight for freedom behind enemy lines, no doubt inspired by an acid-tongue movie critic.

READY EDDIE

The dark figure slid silently down a rope alongside a three story house and swung itself quietly through an open French window on the second floor. The room was pitch black, but the figure moved swiftly through the dark knowing exactly where to go. A door opened slightly, and without a pause, the shadow passed through it, down the staircase and through an opened double door that lead into a study. Here, a night light from an adjoining building bathed the floor of the room through a tall undraped window next to a fireplace.

The figure tip-toed cautiously toward a bookcase on the other side of the fireplace. A hand slid carefully across the end of the books until it touched a certain piece of literature.

The book was gently pulled out and laid on the floor. Then a dark sleeve extended itself through the opening of the bookcase and a small clicking sound was heard. At that instant the room became encased in bright lights. Two men in suits and two police officers, standing no more than ten feet away from the bookcase, jumped on the intruder and wrestled him to the floor while one officer quickly handcuffed his hands behind him. A few words were exchanged, and then the figure in black was lead out of the room, through the front door, and into a small police van hidden in the shadows.

Scotland Yard had just sprung a well planned trap to capture one of London's most notorious safecrackers. His name was Eddie Chapman. His days of robbery were over, but his days of helping Great Britain turn the tide against Nazi Germany had just begun.

Chapman was tried and found guilty of numerous counts of break-ins and imprisoned on the Isle of Jersey in the English Channel. Shortly thereafter, the war broke out and the German army began its roll through the lowlands, quickly swallowing up Belgium and then The Netherlands. Soon the Isle of Jersey was captured by the Germans, and Eddie Chapman figured the change in landlords was going to be his ticket off the island.

Almost on the very day the island was captured, Chapman asked to see the commander of the German occupying force. It took little effort on his part to persuade the German officer that he could be of tremendous help to the Germans by becoming a spy for them.

His cat burglar skills were unmatched and his reputation for getting into files and safes undetected was legendary. His explanation for being in prison was that he was set-up by a beautiful woman. Being set-up was partially true, but the part about the beautiful woman was pure fiction. Chapman felt he might as well add a little spice to the story to make it more interesting. Also, he said he wanted to get back at the British for what they did to him.

Chapman was released, sent to Germany and trained by the *Abwehr*, the Nazi's top spy school. After a few months of rigorous training, Chapman was ready for his first assignment. The Germans must have thought of him as one of the best they had prepared, because the ex-safecracker was to be sent back into the heart of Great Britain to handle a special task: sabotage.

On a cold moon-less night, a German bomber departed from the regular formation of aircraft headed for a night raid on

London and headed out over the English countryside to a point about one hundred miles to the south. Undetected, and alone, the bomber dropped to six thousand feet and Chapman bailed out, parachuting quietly to the ground and landing in an open field. He didn't gather up his chute and escape into the brush as he was trained, but rather stood around waiting for someone to come and capture him. Nothing happened. He walked down a deserted road whistling and then singing. A dog barked, but that was it. Finally he walked into a farm house and surrendered.

Confronted by British military officials, Chapman had a little more difficult time convincing the British than he did the Germans about wanting to become their spy now.

His reputation, known only too well by Scotland Yard, preceded him. Finally, they gave the smooth talker a chance to become a double agent. The Germans thought he was on their side when in fact he was now working for the British. Needless to say, he was being watched very closely by both sides.

Some of Chapman's early assignments as a double agent were radioing back false information to the Germans. Small stuff at first until the British knew the Germans were taking the bait and didn't suspect anything. Then came the major jobs. Among those were sending back reports of damaging air strikes by the German V-2 rockets, when in fact there was no damage, because he had purposely given the Germans incorrect information on where to aim missiles.

Then came the moment Chapman had been trained for by the Germans. He was given his first major sabotage assignment: a large aircraft factory the German air force found difficult to bomb. Destroyed it would drastically curtail Britain's air strikes into the heart of Germany.

Working with British Intelligence, Chapman played an informative role in designing an elaborate camouflage to be draped over the huge factory to make it appear from the air it had been destroyed by sabotage. Installed under the cover of night, it was so convincing that the allies called it one of the most effective deceptions of the war.

The German high command was elated when they viewed their air photos showing the aircraft plant in ruins. They were so impressed they radioed Chapman and informed him he was going to be awarded the Iron Cross. When the war finally ended the former burglar got what he really wanted: a pardon. And with it came the Order of the British Empire.

Eddie Chapman never went back to safe cracking. He worked at odd jobs and enjoyed hanging around in pubs basking in the personal glory of what he did for his country. Before he died in 1972 at the age 66, he was asked by a reporter what he thought was the crowning point of his career as a double agent. He didn't hesitate with his answer. He said it was when actor Christopher Plummer portrayed him in the 1967 movie *Triple Cross*.

A MISSING MEDAL OF HONOR

On September 18, 1942, the American Liberty Ship *S.S. Stephen Hopkins* weighed anchor from Capetown, South Africa, and headed for New Guyana to pick up a cargo of badly needed war materials to take back to the United States. Little did the crew know they were about to be engaged in the war's only one-on-one sea battle of its kind.

The *Hopkins* was launched in Richmond, California, on April 14, 1942, and soon after set sail on its maiden voyage for Australia. After its arrival, the *Hopkins* replaced another Liberty, the *S.S. Robert P. Harper*, to deliver a load of grain to South Africa. The trip was long and hazardous. Severe storms lashed at the ship, driving her off course and causing great damage. She finally made it into Capetown in such battered condition that it would take weeks of valuable time to get the ship seaworthy again. Then on September 18, the *Hopkins* was ordered to New Guyana to pick up a load of bauxite that would be used back home to make aluminum for American aircraft.

After picking up her cargo, and on her return voyage to the United States, the *Hopkins* was only a few days out of Capetown when she ran into heavy fog and rain. Visibility was so poor that the lookouts could hardly see the bow from the bridge. It was during this time that she received a radio message warning that the German raider, *Stier*, was in the vicinity. Before the *Hopkins* could alter her course to escape, the fog suddenly lifted and there looming up only a few hundred yards away was the huge German warship. Crews on both vessels were startled. The *Stier* immediately signaled the *Hopkins* to stop, but the Liberty Ship ignored the warning and swung to port in order to bring her only big gun to face the raider.

One can almost know what the German crew must have been thinking. This was going to be the biggest mismatch in naval warfare. The odds were impossible. The *Hopkins* had one World War I vintage 4" gun, two 37-mm antiaircraft guns, and six machine guns. The *Stier* was armed with six big 5.9" guns, a variety of rapid-firing guns, numerous 30-mm and 50-mm machine guns and several torpedoes. The only thing the crew of the *Hopkins* had going for it was the bravery and in-your-face attitude of a small contingent of navy Armed Guard gunners and a determined group of Merchant Mariners.

The battle raged almost point-blank. The overwhelming gun fire from the German warship ripped into the *Hopkins*, immediately killing crew members and setting fire to the main structure. The navy gunners blasted the bridge of the *Stier* and strafed her decks with machine guns, but they were no match for the awesome salvos coming from the raider. Within minutes, the *Hopkins* was ablaze and sinking. All members of the Armed Guard gun crews were killed, and as the captain gave the order to abandon ship he fell over dead from his wounds. What survivors were left poured over the side into a lifeboat — all except Merchant Marine Cadet Edwin O'Hara.

O'Hara had been helping pass ammunition to the 4-inch gun crew when it was destroyed by a direct hit. Wounded, he staggered up into the damaged gun platform and found all of the gunners dead. The gun, amazingly, was still in firing condition and there were still five rounds available. Having only read how a 4-inch gun works, O'Hara jammed home a round and took aim on the *Stier.*

As fast as he could load, O'Hara fired one round after another at the German ship scoring five devastating direct hits. Shrapnel from the return fire struck O'Hara and he slumped beside his gun bleeding. Within minutes he died, but not until his heroic effort had inflicted heavy damage to the raider. The *Hopkins* went down with 41 Merchant Seamen and 15 Navy Armed Guardsmen. The *Stier* suffered heavy casualties, and was so badly damaged that it had to be scuttled. More than 300 seamen were taken off the stricken German vessel by another raider ship that had been patrolling several miles away.

Thirty-one days later, 15 seamen from the *Hopkins* were found huddled together in a lifeboat that had drifted ashore on a remote beach in Brazil. They gave testimonial to O'Hara's extraordinary action in single-handedly sinking the heavy-armed German raider. No merchant ship in the history of the United States had ever sunk an enemy warship, let alone by one person who had never fired a long-range gun before.

Strangely, O'Hara's gallantry was ignored by the U.S. government. Even the German captain of the *Stier* gave praise to the crew of the *Hopkins* and especially to the lone American seaman who bravely gave his life by firing upon and sinking his ship: more than enough evidence to award the young merchant marine cadet the Congressional Medal of Honor for "conspicuous gallantry above and beyond the call of duty." His name was turned down despite a Presidential order that Merchant Mariners were to receive the citation on the same basis as those in the military.

At the U.S. Merchant Marine Academy at Kings Point, New York, they haven't forgotten Cadet Edwin O'Hara. Hanging in a place of honor is a painting of O'Hara firing the last shot from the *Hopkins.*

And hanging over the painting for more than half-a-century is still a cloud of mystery about why he wasn't considered for the Congressional Medal of Honor.

THE SEAGULL

During World War I, America's top combat pilot against the Germans was Eddie Rickenbacker. In those days, fighter pilots didn't wear parachutes and they flew in something that resembled an orange crate with wings. They couldn't write enough good things about Rickenbacker, even if some of his exploits were stretched a little in the popular dime novels of the time. Nobody really cared. He was a hero and America took to her heroes like nobody else in the world.

The entry of the United States into the Second World War found Rickenbacker too old to serve in the military. He was 51, and like millions of his fellow Americans at that time, he wanted desperately to help out in some way. Since he had been a successful pilot in the first war he felt he could contribute some way in the field of aviation. This made him a perfect fit as a civilian observer under Army Air Force General "Hap" Arnold. And he wasn't going to settle for anything less than being overseas and getting into the thick of the fight. He got his wish and was sent to the Pacific war zone.

In mid-October of 1942, Rickenbacker was aboard a B-17 when it crashed in the Pacific.

He and his crew scrambled into a life raft knowing that land was too far away, and that being rescued by air or ship seemed practically impossible. After being adrift a week, they ran out of water. A few days later the rations were gone. Their thirst was quenched occasionally when they were able to catch rainwater in their hats. When more than two weeks had gone by, their hope for survival began to vanish.

Then something odd happened. A seagull landed on Rickenbacker's head, and in a stillness that seemed frozen in time, he slowly reached up and grabbed the bird. The raw nourishment from the seagull maintained the occupants in the raft until they were saved on November 11th, twenty-seven days after they had plunged into the sea.

What was strange about the event was that there was only one seagull that appeared. There was no sign of others, and the raft was hundreds, or maybe a thousand, miles away from any land. Also, there were no ships anywhere near their vicinity. Seagulls tend to stay close to land or ships and generally remain in flocks.

The Rickenbacker story made headlines across the top of the nation's newspapers. The tale of a courageous survival was what the country needed in late 1942. Rickenbacker was honored, but the WWI ace insisted on sharing the limelight with his surviving crew members. There probably isn't anyone from that generation who doesn't remember those extraordinary circumstances. A movie based on the incident, *Captain Eddie,* was released in 1945 starring Fred McMurray as Rickenbacker.

But the story doesn't end here. It would be another thirty-one years before it did.

In a Florida coast community, decades removed from the end of the war, a lone figure of an old man would walk every morning to the end of a landing near the ocean to feed the seagulls. Residents of the area said the old man was always by himself and seagulls by the hundreds would suddenly appear and flock around him. For years, no one knew who he was, so not much attention was given to his morning ritual. After all, what was so out of the ordinary in seeing a senior citizen standing along a beach feeding seagulls?

Then one day in 1973, the feeding came to a stop. The old man didn't show up and neither did the seagulls. The following day a story appeared in the nation's newspapers that Eddie Rickenbacker had died at the age of 83. Thus ended an old man's daily homage to provide food to seagulls in memory of the one seagull, so long ago, that had miraculously come from out of nowhere to provide the food that would save his life and those of his B-17 crew.

IN A SPLASH OF GLORY

On a sunny fall afternoon in 1942, I was practicing with my high school football team, when suddenly somebody noticed an unusual looking aircraft in the sky to the west of us approaching very low and at a high- rate of speed. We all stopped what we were doing and stared at it in silent awe as it quickly swept over us, dipping its wings, and swiftly disappearing to the east. It was here and gone in a matter of seconds.

We had just experienced an exhilarating close-encounter with the exciting new-looking P-38 fighter plane. I'll never forget it.

The P-38 would become one of the most popular American fighter planes of World War II. With its sleek twin fuselages it became the glamour aircraft of the U.S. Army Air Force. But the P-38 was more than just a classy looking aircraft. It also had great speed, range and firepower. And it played a part in one of the most bizarre incidents of the war involving the downing of an enemy aircraft.

When the P-38 first showed up in the Pacific theater of war it was in late 1942. Air Force General George C. Kenney, who commanded all the Air Force units in the southwest Pacific, was so taken by the aircraft that he made an offer to the pilots àssigned to the new plane. He promised an Air Medal to the first P-38 pilot to bring down a Japanese Zero, which was recognized as one of the finest fighter planes ever built. All the pilots took up the challenge, but none was more dedicated to being the first one to collect that medal than U.S. Army Air Force captain Robert Faurot.

Not long after Faurot took possession of his new P-38, he was assigned to a squadron to attack the Japanese air base at Lae. Just as he peeled off to drop his bomb load on the base he saw a Japanese Zero begin its takeoff on the runway. All Faurot could see in front of his eyes was the Air Medal. This was his chance.

But as his descent toward the Zero quickly reached 2,000 feet, he suddenly remembered he was carrying two 500-pound bombs. He knew that being weighed down with the heavy bombs would seriously hinder his ability to conduct aerial combat with the Zero. He unloaded the bombs, and then pulled up fast so he would escape the blast. He hoped maybe at least the bombs might strike the Zero in its takeoff. He cursed when he realized the bombs weren't going to come close to hitting the enemy plane. In fact, the bombs weren't even going to hit the runway.

Then the impossible happened.

Faurot's two bombs did, in fact, miss the runway. Instead, they landed in the water at the end of the runway causing such a huge water column that when the Zero was just reaching liftoff it hit the huge wave head-on and was knocked into the sea. Faurot couldn't believe his eyes. He had brought down a Zero with water.

Upon returning to his base, Faurot had the other pilots who were in on the raid vouch for the way he brought down the Zero. At first, General Kenney thought it was a gag and wasn't particularly amused. Then he thought it over. Nobody, especially a whole squadron of pilots, could possibly make up such a loony story together and pass it off as being true in order for one guy to get a medal. Also, the general was reminded, in respectful terms, of course, that in his promise regarding the Zero he had said "down" not "shot down."

After having to endure much kidding from General Kenney, Faurot was finally awarded the Air Medal for being the first P-38 pilot to down a Japanese Zero, even if he didn't actually shoot it down.

———————————

An interesting side-note to this story occurred fifty-two years later at my high school's Old Timer's Class Reunion, where anybody who ever attended the school was invited.

I was relating the part of the story about the P-38 zooming low over the football field to a former student five years my senior when suddenly a big grin spread across his face.

"I didn't think anyone would ever remember that," he said. "I was stationed at an air base up north and was a little homesick, so I thought I would just fly home and buzz the old football field. Man, I could have been court-marshaled."

SKOL!

The winner of the Nobel Prize in 1922 was the highly respected Danish physicist, Niels Bohr. He was right out of central casting: uncombed hair, wire-rim glasses and a cheap suit that surely must have also served as his pajamas. Absent minded, too? Of course.

But his brilliance in the early studies of atomic energy was second to none.

When Germany invaded Denmark in 1940, almost everyone who was anyone in the country was thrown behind bars, or put away in concentration camps. Bohr, however, was the exception. The Nazis were willing to put up with his eccentric behavior in exchange for his expertise in atomic research. He was spared, and was allowed to continue with his work under the watchful eye of the dreaded Gestapo.

Bohr didn't skip a beat. He went about his studies as though the German occupation of his country didn't matter, as long as it didn't interfere with his work. This suited the Nazis fine. The Danish scientist never caused any trouble and was left alone with his research, which was certainly going to benefit The Third Reich: a win-win situation all the way around. At least that's the way it appeared on the surface.

Beneath Bohr's rumpled exterior beat the heart of a Danish patriot. By shuffling about his laboratory and burying himself among piles of papers, he conned the Nazis into relaxing a little while he quietly planned his escape. It wasn't going to be easy. He had to find fellow Danes he could trust who would somehow lead him to the right contact that would get him to England.

Three years would pass before he finally put it all together. He figured he couldn't carry all his research papers with him, so he memorized the important parts. But he needed to take a bottle of heavy water, which was crucial to the research and the development of atomic weapons. This would pose a problem if he was captured during his escape and the Germans got a hold of the heavy water. Being a genius, his light bulb went on.

He loved beer and the Germans always kept him well supplied in order to keep him happy. Bohr went to his refrigerator, emptied the contents of one bottle down the drain, and then poured in its place the heavy water. He capped the bottle tightly and placed it back in the refrigerator. When it was time to go he would pack the bottle, and if he was caught the Germans would think it was actually beer. In the meantime, the decoy bottle would remain in the refrigerator, and if the Germans decided to search his room and saw the bottle, they wouldn't think anything different. If he succeeded in escaping, or was caught, one way or the other, the valuable heavy water would be kept from falling into German hands. What a mind!

It was a dark night in the summer of 1943 when a member of the Danish underground knocked gently on Bohr's door. Everything was ready. It was time to go now. The scientist grabbed what few belongings he had already packed, his hat and wrinkled jacket, and was out the door and half way down the stairs when he suddenly stopped. The beer bottle! The one with the heavy water. Much to the surprise of his companion, Bohr darted back up the stairs, flew through his room and swung open the door to the refrigerator. He grabbed the bottle, stuffed it in among his packed clothing, and was soon back down the stairs where his Danish companion must have been having a heart attack. They quickly slipped into the shadows, just missing the Gestapo who had gotten wind that Bohr was planning an escape.

Making their way on foot into the Danish country side, they met up with two more members of the underground who escorted the scientist through a wooded area next to an open field. A few lights blinked and soon a small aircraft floated down on to the dark field. In a matter of seconds, Bohr was whisked aboard the plane and in the air heading for England. He smiled as the aircraft skimmed undetected over the English Channel. He had pulled it off. It took three years, but he had out-smarted the Nazis by being his usual eccentric self with a phony who-cares attitude toward their occupation of his homeland. Now he was going to fight back. The Allies were going to have his atomic knowledge to bring down the hated Nazi regime and free his beloved Denmark.

When Bohr arrived in England, he was met by a British staff car and driven immediately to a countryside manor. Here he was met by military personnel and top members of the British scientific community. He was applauded for his three years of patient planning and daring escape. And he was especially commended for his many atomic research achievements and his ability to keep the crucial details out of German hands; truly, one of the most courageous acts of World War II.

When Bohr retired that evening he unpacked his bundle of clothing and out rolled the decoy bottle of beer with the heavy water. He had almost forgotten about it. He grinned when he thought how his colleagues would embrace him again. It was the most critical part of his atomic research. Then he took a closer look.

In his haste to escape he had grabbed an actual bottle of beer.

A SPECIAL OLD GLORY

Some years back my wife and I went on a tour of Washington, D.C. We both agreed that one of the highlights of trip was visiting the Smithsonian Institute. Not having ever seriously read up on the famous museum, we expected it to be one big building and not several that would take you at least a week to go through. We didn't have that much time, but we were able to explore at least three of the buildings.

I'll never forget the first building we entered. We walked through the front doors and there standing suddenly before us was a huge American flag. It almost took our breath away. It was tattered and faded, but hung proudly against the wall as if at attention. Within its presence everyone stood in quiet reverence gazing at the awesome sight trying to grasp the notion that what they were witnessing was the beginning of the United States.

Hanging there was the actual American flag that Francis Scott Keyes viewed from his captivity aboard a British warship when he wrote the *Star Spangled Banner*.

I never forgot that sight, and I have often wondered about other American flags. Did they also have stories to tell about our country? I did a little research on the subject, received a few emails from friends across the country, and from this I was able to uncover some interesting tales. This is just one of them.

I think the flag story that intrigued me the most concerns the flag that was flying over the nation's Capitol Building on

December 7, 1941, the day the Japanese struck Pearl Harbor, bringing the United States into a global war.

Two and one-half years later, on June 4, 1944, American forces entered Rome by pushing the Germans back into northern Italy. It was the first major enemy city to surrender to the Allies. To celebrate the victory, President Roosevelt had the Capitol Building flag hauled down and sent to the American military command in Rome for it to be raised over the captured Italian city. It would be the first of many stops for this special Old Glory.

In July of 1945, Berlin fell to the Allied forces ending the Nazi reign of terror. The flag was taken down over Rome and sent to Germany where on July 20 it was run up the flag pole over the German capitol. Later it was flown to the Pacific war zone.

When Guam was recaptured from the Japanese, the same flag was hoisted over the island's American military headquarters. Then when the Japanese were defeated at Iwo Jima it was flown there to mark the victory. Soon it was flying over Okinawa as American forces inched closer to the Japanese mainland.

The flag's greatest moment, however, came on September 2, 1945 when it flew high atop the *U.S.S Missouri* during the Japanese surrender ceremonies. Five days later, on September 7, General Douglas McArthur requested that the flag be sent to Tokyo to fly over that city.

As the American occupation of Japan began to settle in, the flag was quietly hauled down and shipped back to Washington, D.C. where it resumed its original position flying high above the nation's Capitol Building as our symbol of freedom.

THE STRANGER

I hadn't been in my office ten minutes one morning, when I received a telephone call from a lady who was obviously a little nervous about talking to me. She began by saying she was coaxed by family members to call me and relate a strange experience she had pertaining to World War II. She added that I would probably think she was crazy, but it was something that had haunted her, especially for the last twelve years. I could use her story, she said, but she wasn't going to give me names. I could use her first name, which was Claire. I agreed, then she proceeded to tell me her story.

It was one of the most mysterious and fascinating tales I have ever heard.

When Claire was a young girl about twelve years old, she lived in Hawaii. Home was a small white house in a small town just outside of Honolulu. Her father worked in a lumber shop while her mother raised three children and did odd jobs to add to their income. An aunt also lived with them, and was dating an American sailor stationed aboard the battleship *Oklahoma* at Pearl Harbor. The two had quickly fallen in love, and within a couple of weeks announced they wanted to get married. Not knowing how long his ship would be anchored at Pearl Harbor, they decided to have a small wedding as soon as possible. They planned it for a Sunday afternoon, which would be ten days away. This would give them time to fill out what papers were needed, and for the young sailor to do the same through naval authorities. The wedding date would be December 7, 1941.

On the day before the wedding, Claire's parents threw a yard party for the soon-to-be-married couple and invited almost everyone they knew. The adults were milling around greeting friends they hadn't seen for sometime, and children were laughing and darting in and out of the house. There was plenty of food, beer and ice cream to go around for everyone. The sound of guitars and singing made it a festive occasion Claire would never forget, especially with what was about to happen.

In amongst the crowd, she noticed a hatless, gray haired man in a light tan topcoat who seemed oddly out of place. He was standing off to one side talking to her aunt's young sailor beau. What caught Claire's attention, she remembers, was that there was no rain in sight and it was just warm enough that day for the men to be wearing casual shirts and the women lightweight dresses. The stranger and the sailor talked for some time and then Claire's aunt joined them. The three strolled around to the side of the house carrying on a quiet conversation until Claire's mother noticed them. She started toward them when the stranger shook the sailor's hand, said something to both of them, and then turned away to walk toward the road. What happened next, Claire said, was the beginning of a string of mysterious incidents she would never be able to get out of her mind.

The stranger smiled at Claire, and as he passed by he greeted her by softly saying her name. She remembers it startled her a little, because how did this complete stranger know her name? He kept walking away until he reached the road and stood at a bus stop. Claire noticed he kept staring back at the party until a small bus arrived. She watched him get on the bus, and then it slowly drove away. Nobody at the party knew who he was.

As the party began to break up, Claire remembers being in the house and seeing the young sailor talking on the telephone. She heard her aunt say to her mother that he wasn't going back to his ship that evening because he was sick with "food poisoning." Later on, he stretched out on the davenport, and that's where Claire remembers him staying all night.

The next morning she recalls being in the kitchen when there was suddenly a commotion everywhere. Out in front of the house she remembers her dad and the sailor talking and looking toward some huge black clouds rising in the distance. It was not long before somebody in the road in front of Claire's house told them Pearl Harbor had been bombed. Then she overheard the sailor saying something to her aunt, and then driving off with her dad in his car. It would be later on that they found out the battleship *Oklahoma* was one of the many navy ships destroyed that morning in an air raid by the Japanese.

The sailor eventually made it back to Pearl Harbor and helped with the injured in the aftermath of the attack. He had been spared from possibly being killed. Hundreds of sailors on the *Oklahoma* alone lost their lives that Sunday. Claire doesn't remember much more after that except her aunt and the sailor didn't get married until 1943, and after the war lived in Texas somewhere. In 1981 her aunt died. It was then that Claire's mother told her the story about the stranger at the party.

The gray haired man in the tan topcoat had walked up to the sailor and told him he shouldn't go back to Pearl Harbor that evening because his ship was going to be destroyed in an air attack by the Japanese the next morning. The sailor laughed. You mean this guy can see in the future? But Claire's aunt became worried. Maybe he was a nut, but he seemed strangely convincing.

After some more conversation, the stranger left the party. Then with much insistence from the aunt, the sailor reluctantly telephoned an officer on the *Oklahoma* saying he was sick with "food poisoning" from the party and couldn't make it back. The lie worked, and he was granted permission not to come back aboard ship that night. The officer knew he was getting married the next day, and hoped he would be well enough to stand up before the preacher. Then the attack occurred in the morning and the sailor was safe because he was warned to stay away from his ship by a weird stranger. Claire's aunt and her sailor almost went into shock. Who was this stranger, where did he come from, and how could he possibly predict what was going to happen? And why did he choose this sailor to save? Maybe it was a strange coincidence. Whatever it was, the two never spoke about the incident again to anyone except to Claire's mother and father.

I told Claire this was an incredible story. Unexplained things like this occur all the time.

Then came a pause in our telephone conversation.

"Mr. Merrill," Claire finally said, "believe it or not, this isn't the end of the story."

She continued by saying her mother and father both passed away in 1985, and after her aunt had died in 1988, her husband, the sailor, moved to Oakland, California. Here he lived alone, not far from Claire, until he died in the summer of 1990. She said she went to his funeral and then attended the military graveside service afterwards. It was here she met a couple of men who had been his shipmates aboard the _Oklahoma._ It was a sad but comforting moment. She wasn't prepared, however, for what happened next.

At the conclusion of the graveside service, she turned to walk back up a grassy knoll to her car when she noticed a man standing next to another car. He was hatless, gray haired and wearing a tan topcoat. Claire said she stopped dead in her tracks. Her knees suddenly felt weak, her throat went dry and her heart started to pound wildly. She swore she was going to faint. He stood there staring at her as she tried to move. It was him, she was positive. He hadn't aged a minute. But how could it be him? That was nearly fifty years ago. Her mind must be playing tricks.

She was now no more than a few feet from the stranger when he said softly, "He had a good and full life, didn't he, Claire?"

Claire said she stood paralyzed as the stranger turned, got in his car and slowly drove away.

———————————

To add further mystery to this story, Claire abruptly ended our telephone conversation saying she had to hang up because she was going to be late for an appointment with her daughter-in-law. She promised she would call me back about mid-afternoon. She never did. She never revealed her last name, nor was I able to get her telephone number. There was no way I could tell by the telephone I was using whether it was a local or long distance call. Maybe Claire wasn't even her real name. The only thing I had for sure was that she must now be about seventy three years old and probably living in the Oakland, California area. She did tell me something, however, that even adds more to the mystery.

The license plate on the car the stranger drove away in read: "U.S. Government."

NOT A LEG TO STAND ON

When Hitler invaded Poland in 1939, Great Britain quickly declared war on Germany. The Nazis, who had been building their giant war machine for nearly ten years, crushed the Poles in a matter of weeks. The British were slow to mobilize, and her air force especially wasn't prepared to handle the strength of the German Luftwaffe. Plenty of British fighter planes were rolling out of English assembly plants, but there was a serious shortage of qualified pilots to fly them.

Among those answering the urgent call for experienced aviators was an ex-Royal Air Force pilot by the name of Douglas Bader. The thirty year old, who had survived an air crash in 1931, desperately wanted to be reinstated in order to serve his country. At first, there was some hesitation on the part of the R.A.F, but when Bader passed the qualifying tests, and proved he could handle a Spitfire fighter plane better than most, he was given his wings and put into action. About this time the German army had swept through the low lands and was conquering France.

As the war progressed, Bader eventually was given command of the 242nd Squadron and soon became one of Britain's most successful fighter pilots. During 1940 and 1941, he wreaked havoc on the German air force by shooting down 22 of their aircraft. He became the war hero the British so badly needed at this particular stage of the fighting. Bestowed upon him were the bars of the Distinguished Service Order and the Distinguished Flying Cross. Only the third person to be so decorated.

Then on August 9, 1941, during a mission over the European continent, Bader's squadron tangled head-on with several German planes. It turned into a bitter dogfight. Bader wasted no time in sending one enemy aircraft down in flames, and was getting in behind another for the kill, when he was side-swiped by a German ME109. The Spitfire started spinning out of control and Bader had only one chance to survive. He quickly bailed out and plunged to about one hundred feet above the ground before opening his parachute so he could escape the falling Spitfire. He landed safely on a country road, but before his chute could be unbuckled, he found himself looking down the barrel of a German rifle.

Bader was taken immediately to a prison camp inside Germany. While he was there, he attempted several escapes, but on each occasion was captured and drug back and thrown into solitary confinement. The feisty pilot was such a nuisance the Germans finally took him away and imprisoned him in the dreaded Colditz Castle prison. This was the big lock-up for those certain Allied prisoners-of-war who kept refusing to play by the German rules. Bader found his new home impossible to escape from, so he remained there as a guest of the Germans until the end of the war.

Douglas Bader's accomplishments during World War II were extraordinary. None more, however, than the obstacle he had to overcome to convince the R.A.F at the beginning of the war he was ready to fly Spitfires against the enemy and become one of Great Britain's greatest war heroes.

Remember the 1931 air crash we mentioned in the beginning? The reason Bader was released from the R.A.F back then was because he had lost both his legs in the crash.

COKE GOES TO WAR

When American youth marched off to war, so did a lot of businesses. For example, major auto makers turned their plants into making tanks and airplanes, and clothing manufacturers switched to turning out uniforms for all branches of the military.

Even a cigarette company got in step. Lucky Strikes for decades had been packed in a dark green package, and in 1942 it turned white, so that the green dye in the printing could be used in military camouflage. How much of this is actually true, I'm not sure. But it did made a great advertising slogan: "Lucky Strike green has gone to war."

But I think the role Coca Cola played in the war was probably the most interesting, and it wasn't because of anything the soft drink company had in mind.

On December 7, 1941, when the Japanese bombed Pearl Harbor, the attack was so swift and devastating that the medical supplies aboard the target navy ships were destroyed.

Casualties were staggering. An urgent call went out to survivors in the harbor for blood donors, and as they came forward the medics were suddenly faced with a critical emergency. They were running out of the usual blood containers. Then somebody got a bright idea. They gathered up all the Cokes they could find, emptied the bottles and sterilized them, and then used the bottles to store the blood. No doubt many lives were saved.

Two weeks later, as the Japanese were over-running the Philippines, the U.S. Army found itself woefully out numbered and without much means to stop the invaders. Japanese tanks rolled almost unchecked against the American defenses. Then an American army private by the name of Soria stepped up with a plan that might at least slow down the enemy tanks. He and some of his buddies went through an abandoned PX building and gathered up all the Coke bottles they could find. Then they used them to make as many Molotov cocktails as they could to throw at the tanks. Many claimed this tactic slowed the Japanese advance enough to allow the defending U.S. Army to retreat from Batann to the island of Corregidor.

When Richard Bong, American's top flying ace, shot down his twenty-sixth enemy aircraft he had just surpassed Eddie Rickenbacker's World War I record. This called for a celebration. General Douglas MacArthur and a number of his staff met with Bong and broke out the champagne to toast the war hero for his accomplishment. Then Bong put a slight damper on the event. He told MacArthur he was a teetotaler, but he could sure use a Coke. After a short delay, and a little scurrying around, a case of Coca Cola arrived and MacArthur resumed his toast to Bong.

There is also a story about two U.S. Army privates playing a game of checkers during a lull in the fighting somewhere in Belgium. They made a chess board out of a piece of plywood and used full Coca Cola bottles for the checkers. The one making the most jumps, of course, would get the most Cokes and be declared the winner. There was, however, a slight change in their rules. When a king was crowned the one being crowned had to down the whole bottle before they could proceed. Meaning, you could be winning and still lose if too much Coca

Cola was consumed and you became too sick to continue. No wonder we won the war?

Perhaps the most interesting use of the Coca Cola bottle during the war was by President Jimmy Carter. The future President was getting ready to enter the Naval Academy in 1943 when he became a little nervous about not being accepted because of his flat feet. So, every day for weeks leading up to his physical examination, he would roll his feet on Coke bottles.

Evidently it worked.

A TREE GROWS FOR CROMWELL

The Congressional Medal of Honor is the highest commendation the United States can bestow on its war heroes. The citation reads: *"…for conspicuous gallantry and intrepidity at the risk of life and above and beyond the call to duty."*

There are many ways our nation pays homage to the recipients of this great honor, but there are probably none more impressive than the special 52 acre grove of trees adjacent to historic Valley Forge Park known as Medal of Honor Grove. It has to be one of the best kept secrets in America. My wife and I were on a tour many years ago that took us to Valley Forge Park, but nothing was ever mentioned to the tour group about the Medal of Honor Grove. It would be fifteen years later before I would first hear about the grove.

In this picturesque setting, each recipient of the citation has a tree named in his honor with a stainless steel marker identifying who he is and the date and location of his heroic achievement. But the centerpiece of this patriotic forest is an acre of trees that have been set aside for each state of the union. All together, the trees, if you were looking down on them from above, form a geographic shape of the United States with each acre displaying a 7' 7" obelisk designed in the shape of the Washington Monument. Here the names of the recipients of the Medal of Honor from that particular state are inscribed.

None was more deserving of our country's highest award than John Philip Cromwell. What he did to earn this honor during World War II, for some reason, is little-known. Audie Murphy, our most decorated hero of WWII, once said Cromwell's act of heroism was one of the most courageous he had ever heard about. He was often surprised that no one else seemed to have much knowledge about Cromwell and the great sacrifice he made for his country.

The forty-three year old Cromwell was commander of the Division 43 Submarine Coordinated Attack Group in the South Pacific during the early stages of the war. As captain of the flag ship submarine _Sculpin,_ Cromwell's mission was to prowl these Japanese -controlled waters, not only to seek out and destroy enemy shipping, but to report any enemy movement and military build-up in the region. He was also privy to some very top secret information.

Being the captain of the task force, Cromwell was the only one outside the military high command who possessed all the secret intelligence information concerning the United States submarine strategy and tactics in the South Pacific. This also included U.S. warship movements and specific attack plans.

In mid- November of 1943, Cromwell set out with his undersea flotilla to probe the enemy stronghold at Truk Island prior to the U.S. invasion. It was a treacherous mission. Two Japanese destroyers almost immediately detected the submarines and zeroed in on the first one in their sights. It was the _Sculpin._

Depth charges pounded the submarine repeatedly, causing such extreme damage that Cromwell took the _Sculpin_ down deeper to avoid the onslaught. But it was too late. They were taking on water. He quickly ordered the submarine to the surface to take on the two enemy ships in a gunfight. Cromwell knew the _Sculpin's_ one deck gun would be no match for the superior firepower of the Japanese destroyers, but the encounter would give him the opportunity he needed to order his crew to abandon ship. The one-sided battle was over in minutes, and the crew was able to escape the doomed vessel on rafts.

Then, according to those who survived the ordeal, and lived to tell the story, a cool and undaunted Captain Cromwell remained alone aboard the submarine as it slowly sank below the surface to its watery grave.

Cromwell purposely sacrificed himself rather than be captured by the Japanese and be tortured, or drugged, into revealing the secret naval plans he possessed. If he had given himself up to the Japanese, the war in the Pacific might have taken a different course entirely.

Today, a tree stands for John Philip Cromwell in the Medal of Honor Grove because he, like many of those so honored with him, exhibited great courage in the face of certain death to protect man's highest aspiration — freedom.

THE MIRACLE

In preparing for this book, and the video documentaries I produce, I have been able to accumulate an incredible file of stories that make up a remarkable history of World War II.

The material comes from my research in libraries, contacts with military history buffs and letters or emails from countless service veterans and their families from all over America. It stared in 1996 when I produced my first WWII video, *Forgotten Valor*. It's been an exciting labor of love ever since.

Not long ago, I was asked by a WWII veteran friend of mine that with all this information I've obtained, what, in my opinion, was the most defining moment of the war. How can anyone really answer that question? I told him there were so many great battles fought and won that any one of them could have been pivotal in winning the war. I thought about it for several days, and while I was digging through my files pertaining to another matter, I came across some information I had used in a segment for one of the documentaries. I read it over and once again I shook my head in disbelief. What I was looking at had to be proof that this was truly the event. Some historians have called it the miracle of the twentieth century.

Following December 7, 1941, nobody was so totally unprepared to fight a war than the United States. Only a month before, our army had been on maneuvers using pick-up trucks to simulate tanks. In 1940, our arms production didn't exist, and in early 1941 a National Guard unit was ordered to guard the mouth of the Columbia River with a machine gun.

When the Japanese surprised us at Pearl Harbor, they virtually wiped out the U.S. Pacific fleet. Our air power in that region was also erased. On that Sunday morning, in less than two hours, 18 warships were lost, 347 aircraft either destroyed or damaged, and nearly 2,500 were dead. The navy lost almost three times as many men as in the Spanish American War and World War I combined. Luckily, the U.S. aircraft carriers were away from the harbor on patrol, or the Japanese attack would have been even worse. America was on its knees and bleeding.

Keep in mind where this country stood in the aftermath of Pearl Harbor in comparison to our enemies. The Japanese, who had been fighting wars since 1931, were overrunning everything in their path in the Pacific and Southeast Asia. Germany's awesome military forces had quickly crushed the countries in the low lands of Europe, got France to surrender in something like six weeks, and had Great Britain and Russia teetering on the brink of defeat. In the meantime, Italy had bolstered the Axis strength by invading North Africa along with the Germans, and was rolling toward Egypt. Everything seemed lost for the Allied nations. The end of the free world appeared to be only a matter of time.

Then a sleeping giant began to struggle to its feet. The miracle was about to begin.

The Axis nations had a ten year head start in building their mighty war machines. The United States had its back against the wall and was beginning from a standing start.

What the American people would soon accomplish would astonish the enemy, their Allies and even themselves. Within

These 1943 teenagers participated in an event that has been recognized as the miracle of the 20th century.

two years, the United States arms production equaled that of Germany, Japan and Italy combined. By 1943, U.S. production surpassed the Axis nations by more than 50 percent. In 1944 it was twice as much.

With more the 15 million men and women in the U.S. armed forces, the civilian population was mobilized almost overnight to energize the war production. Nearly 54 million answered the call. Women left their homes to take up the battle in shipyards and aircraft plants, men who were physically unable to serve in the armed forces quit their jobs to do the same, or signed up with the Merchant Marine to deliver war supplies to the fighting forces wherever they were throughout the world. Senior citizens

These two women were part of an army of war workers that turned out a staggering total of U.S. combat aircraft. How many would you guess? (A) 35,000? (B) 180,000? (C) 300,000?

and children went into the fields to help harvest crops and gather scrap metal for the war factories. Then there were those who served on draft boards and rationing boards or became airplane spotters. Most families planted 'victory gardens' in their backyards and in window sill boxes — wherever they could find a spot of ground. More than half of a family's fresh vegetables were produced through victory gardens.

They stood in endless lines almost daily to buy food and shoes with ration stamps. Automobile production ceased in order to make tanks and bombers, while gasoline rationing allowed most citizens only three gallons a week, and women were asked to give up their nylon stockings to make parachutes. They solved that problem by painting their legs.

But what was accomplished in numbers by this home-front army of patriots staggers the imagination, making it almost impossible to comprehend. Nearly 300,000 airplanes were produced, 86,000 tanks, 6,500 navy ships, 5,500 cargo vessels, 65,000 landing craft, 315,000 artillery guns, 17 million rifles and over four million tons of artillery shells. They also found time to give 13 million pints of blood, and turn over ten percent of their pay- check to buy war bonds. A German general once commented after the war that America's industrial might, fueled by its determined citizenry, was too much for the Axis nations to overcome.

What the American people sacrificed and accomplished to support their armed forces in such a short time was indeed the miracle of the twentieth century. I hear comments, even from my generation who were there when all this happened, that the people of the United States today could never rise to that pentacle of united patriotism and sacrifice again.

People are different nowadays, they say.

Don't you believe that for a minute.

SPIES

Spies. The war was infested with them. Novels and movies have found their hidden world of intrigue irresistible in the role they played in deciding the outcome of battles and eventually the war. Here are just two of the many that were considered the best.

Alfred George Owens was a Canadian who became responsible for keeping the Germans from setting up a successful spy ring in Great Britain during the war. His cunning efforts, you would think, would have earned him England's highest medal and gotten him knighted by the king. In fact, it's surprising they didn't hang him.

The day after war was declared in 1939, Owens was picked up by British intelligence agents in London after several months of surveillance proved him to be a German spy.

They sat the Canadian down under a bright light and gave him two choices: either work secretly for the British and make the Germans think he was still on their side, or be hanged. It's obvious what fate he chose, because within an hour he was transmitting British controlled information back to Germany.

Owens was a perfectionist. His messages were so cleverly misleading that the Germans never suspected they were being fed information that would eventually favor the Allies. He even set up a false German spy network in London with branches supposedly in all corners of the British Isles. The Germans fell for it. The Nazi high command had such trust and high praise for Owens that they sent secret agents into

Great Britain at his request to help him operate the spy network. The only thing was, those enemy agents were being picked up the moment they stepped on English soil and whisked off to a prison for interrogation.

Until the day the war ended six years later, the Germans never had a clue that Owens was working for the British and not for them. His record was most remarkable, to say the least, when you consider every spy sent by the Germans into Great Britain during the war was captured. Not one of them made it.

During this time, a cunning operative by the name of Dusko Popov surfaced. The cool and cunning manner in which he handled his daring exploits as a double agent would have a major influence on generations yet to come.

Born in Yugoslavia, Popov became involved in British intelligence during the thirties, under the code name *Tricycle*. When war broke out in Europe in 1939, he became a double agent by first feeding deceptive information given to him by the British to the Germans; then acting as a Nazi spy he would relay vital military movements being conducted by the Germans back to the British. To say he was enthusiastic about his role as a double agent would be an understatement. He was a suave, dashing playboy with an eye for the ladies and a devil-may-care lifestyle. The perfect cover that at times worried those he secretly worked for, especially the British.

Then in early 1941, he was contacted by the Germans to go to America on a special assignment which wouldn't be disclosed to him until after his arrival. He alerted the British, who in turn contacted their contemporaries in the United States about

Popov's secret mission. The green light was then given to Popov to move ahead and make his contact in America. Since the United States was not at war, both countries were a little more than curious about what the German's wanted.

Through a series of telephone messages, Popov finally met up with a German agent who gave him these specific orders: he was to find out all he could about the defenses of Pearl Harbor. This puzzled Popov, because he couldn't figure out why the Germans were so interested in Hawaii which was halfway around the world from them. The only possible reason, he thought, would be that the Germans were going to pass the Pearl Harbor information on to Japan, who at the time was threatening everybody in the Pacific.

At great risk, Popov went directly to J. Edgar Hoover of the FBI and warned him about the special interest Germany was taking in the Hawaiian Islands. He was stunned when Hoover ignored him. When he mentioned Japan's possible involvement in the information his reaction was the same. Popov was shown the door and that was that. So, it wasn't much of a surprise to him when he turned his radio on a few months later and heard the news about the Japanese attack on Pearl Harbor.

Popov continued with his spy work throughout the rest of the war, and when it ended, his character as a handsome international spy, who always stayed one step ahead of enemy agents, became the model for Ian Fleming's James Bond. While he quietly enjoyed this notoriety, it's been said that he was always deeply troubled about why J. Edgar Hoover never took his warning about Pearl Harbor seriously.

MICHAEL'S WAR

Michael Kelly almost ran up the gangway of the Liberty Ship to which he was assigned from the Brooklyn Armed Guard Naval Center. This is what he had been looking forward to since he joined the Navy three months prior. He was finally going to sea and from there see some action.

Michael was just eighteen and his older brother David had already been in the Navy for two years, seeing combat in the South Pacific. He remembers vividly the adulation David received from his parents and neighbors when he came home on his first overseas leave; especially from his father who had been in the Navy on a destroyer during the first war.

To his father, David was a hero with all of his combat ribbons. Michael had only been fifteen when David enlisted, and it was quite obvious to everyone, the older son was the father's favorite. Michael was smaller in stature, and when he enlisted at seventeen he looked more like thirteen. In his father's eyes he would never measure up to David, unless he proved himself in major combat. That's the way it was. And Michael was determined to prove himself, and now that he was in the Navy he was going to get his chance.

The Liberty Ship was tied up at a pier in New York loaded down with airplane fuel, ammunition, and small trucks. It was headed for England and Michael was coming aboard as a signalman attached to the Navy gun crew. The ship was scheduled to leave in four days and Michael wanted to celebrate the event, particularly with his father and brother, who had just arrived home on a short leave.

The afternoon before the day of his departure, Michael met his father and brother David at a small bar in New Jersey where his father hung out every night with his friends. There was lots of toasting, laughter, and storytelling, with some kidding going on about Michael's lack of sea experience, and much boasting about David and his father's combat duty.

Near midnight the three parted company with Michael getting a hug from his brother and a reluctant handshake from his father. Michael watched with envy as the two walked away from him with his father's arm around David's shoulder. He just had to see some action. Only then would things really be different between his father and him.

The following evening, Michael's cargo ship pulled away from the pier and moved slowly through the New York Harbor and past the Statue of Liberty. It was completely dark as the laden down ship started for the open sea. Michael was standing watch on the bridge since he and all the Navy gunners on board were required, as a routine procedure, to be in their combat positions one hour before sunset and one hour afterwards as a precaution against enemy attack.

Michael stood bracing the cold wind as he looked over his shoulder at the lights from the New York skyline which illuminated the horizon. He thought it was odd this should be happening. Wasn't the city supposed to be blacked out? He would learn years later that the city largely ignored the curfew since the enemy was an ocean away and didn't have bombers anywhere near the range to reach them. Maybe not bombers, but they certainly had something else just as sinister lurking beneath the surface.

Micheal was still gazing and pondering about the lighted skyline when suddenly a devastating explosion shook the ship. He was thrown halfway across the bridge against a railing and then saw a body fly over his head. It was unreal how quickly it happened. More explosions followed and the ship started to list dramatically to the port side. Fire raged everywhere and Michael saw men jumping into the sea below him. Nobody was at his gun position as the order came to abandon ship.

Not more than a hundred yards off the starboard side he saw a German submarine surface. He froze in the middle of the nightmare going on around him and stared in disbelief at the sub as three men appeared in the conning tower. He quickly climbed into the vacant 20-millimeter gun tub facing the submarine and strapped himself into position. It was loaded and ready to fire. This was his moment, he thought. He pulled the trigger and a blast of fire strafed the conning tower killing at least two of the men. Two more climbed down from the conning tower and raced for their deck gun, but a spray of gunfire toppled them into the sea. The submarine started to submerge.

Michael unstrapped himself from the 20-millimeter and was climbing out of the gun tub when a horrific blast sent him reeling down the ladder to the next deck. He was bleeding as he tried to make his way down to the main deck and onto the catwalk that had been built over the army trucks that were secured there. Lifeboats were being lowered above him and men from everywhere were trying to climb in. He jumped over the side and landed in the middle of an ocean of burning oil, but he was able to surface through the fire by waving his arms over his head and pushing the flames away from him.

Within minutes he was pulled into a lifeboat filled with surviving merchant seamen and Navy crewmen. While in the lifeboat the Naval officer in charge of the crew praised Michael for his bravery in taking on the German submarine alone and keeping them from inflicting more damage on the survivors. He hinted at a medal or some kind of commendation.

It would be an hour or so before they would be rescued by the Coast Guard. Michael's watch said 10:30 p.m. It would be close to midnight before they were taken ashore and assembled in a large barracks where they were given blankets and hot coffee. Amazingly only three lives were lost. He learned later it took only about ten minutes for the ship to sink.

At 7 a.m. the ones who had escaped serious injury, were taken by truck to the Brooklyn Navy Yard. Michael's bleeding was caused by a cut on his chest, but nothing serious. By noon he had been bandaged, taken a shower, given clean clothes, and fed. Before the afternoon was over he had been given a three-day pass, after which he was to report back to the base for active duty.

It was near 8 p.m. that night when Michael walked though the door of his father's favorite bar in New Jersey. Just as he suspected, his father and brother David were sitting up at the bar. As he approached them, his father turned and faced Michael. His expression was one of astonishment. David's jaw dropped. Neither said a word at first, then Michael finally spoke. He remembers the actual conversation to this day.

"Well, I'm back," Michael said, "and you won't believe what happened."

"What did you do, jump ship?" his bewildered Father asked.

"Well, I went to sea," Michael continued. "My ship was torpedoed by a German sub, I strafed its conning tower and killed maybe three or four guys. I spent hours in a lifeboat. I'm going to get a Purple Heart and maybe another medal for bravery. Is that enough combat for you guys?"

As he turned to walk away he heard his brother say, "But you were just in here last night."

"That's right!" Michael replied with a weariness in his voice, "but right now I'm tired and I got to get some rest."

Michael Kelly walked through the door, called a cab and checked back into the Brooklyn Navy Yard for some well deserved sleep with three more days left on his pass. He had had enough war for one day.

CODES

One of the most fascinating codes devised by the Allies was the one they sent to warn the French Resistance that the Allied invasion was about to start. It's been dramatized many times in movies and television documentaries, but what is little-known about the code is the daring chance the Allies took in the way they transmitted it to the French Resistance.

The message was Paul Verlaine's well-known poem, *Ode to Autumn*. The French Resistance knew beforehand that certain words in the poem meant the location and time of the landings, but weren't quite sure how they would receive the message. It could be by short-wave radio, a courier dropped by parachute into France at night, or even by carrier pigeon. They only knew they would know it when they got the message, regardless of how it was to arrive. And the Allied high command in England *wanted* this important message to be heard by the Germans.

The decision was made to broadcast Verlaine's poem right over BBC for everyone to hear. It has been said that some Allied officials almost choked on the idea. They argued that you might as well call Hitler on the telephone and tell him personally the actual date and time. It was terribly risky, and thousands of lives would be at stake. But the final decision to go ahead was based on the idea of being obvious.

German intelligence heard the poem read over the air, and had no problem figuring out there was a message in there somewhere about an impending invasion. The person who read the poem did so in such a slow and deliberate manner that it made some of the members of the Allied command cringe. He was a little too obvious, they thought, in trying to make sure the Germans didn't miss a word. Precisely the idea, of course, but it was a little more deliberate than they had expected.

The trap door was opened and the Germans fell through it. They couldn't believe the Allies would actually go on radio and announce when and where they were coming ashore. They brushed it off as being a hoax and were amused the Allies would think they would fall for such a dumb trick. Exactly the reaction the Allies had hoped for.

The D-Day invasion went off as planned in the "coded" poem, and a major force of the German troops designated to defend the French coastline remained farther north, away from Normandy. It would be a few days later, after the Allies had secured their beachhead and begun moving inland, that German intelligence would realize they had been had. By then it was too late.

Certainly one of the most commonly used codes of the war among the American troops was the one called the "GI Code." If a military sentry was forced to challenge an unknown intruder he would simply ask them questions like, "Who plays center field for the New York Yankees?" or, "Whose orchestra's theme song is *Moonlight Serenade*?" If they couldn't answer they were in deep trouble.

There is one story concerning the "GI Code," or "GI Quiz," told to me by a Marine veteran that happened during one of the hotly contested battles on an island in the South Pacific. It was night, and a squad of Marines was pinned down in the dense jungle thicket, not knowing exactly where the enemy was located. After hours of silence, they heard a rustling noise a few yards in front of them. The sergeant, who was crouched the closest to the noise, put his finger to his lips for the others not to make a sound.

"Who goes there?" the sergeant asked.

"Dixieland," the answer came back.

The password "Dixieland" was correct, but the sergeant wanted to make sure.

"Who were the brothers who played in *Night at The Opera?*" he said.

A short silence, and then came the reply, "The Malx Blothels!"

The Marines opened fire into the jungle thicket and wiped out seven Japanese soldiers. It was a known fact the Japanese couldn't pronounce "r" in English.

Then there was the American sentry on guard at a road crossing during the Battle of The Bulge. With so many Germans infiltrating U.S. lines disguised as American soldiers at the time, the military police were being extra cautious. When a jeep staff car approached an MP's position, he halted the vehicle and told the other sentries to keep their rifles aimed at the two occupants while he asked the officer to identify himself.

"I'm General Omar Bradley," came the answer.

"If you're General Omar Bradley, then what is the capital of Illinois?"

"Springfield."

"Where is the guard placed on the line of scrimmage?"

"Between the tackle and the center."

"Then who is Betty Grable married to?"

Dead silence. The officer frowned and then answered.

"I don't know who she's married to now, soldier."

The MP ordered the officer and his driver out of the jeep. One of the other sentries nudged him and said that it was *really* General Omar Bradley.

"I know it is," he said, "but he didn't say Harry James."

The MP was promptly reprimanded by an officer nearby, but General Bradley stepped in and commended the soldier for his devotion to duty. He also thanked him for not being trigger-happy and promised he would brush up on who was currently married to whom in Hollywood.

THE SECRET

Michael Thomas was sitting on the back steps of his house watching his Uncle Jim work on his Model A Ford when his dad came out the back door and announced to both of them that he had just heard on the radio that the Japanese had bombed Pearl Harbor. Neither Michael nor his Uncle Jim had ever heard of Pearl Harbor until Michael's dad explained it was in the Hawaiian Islands. That's a long ways away from Kansas City, Michael thought, but he could tell by his dad's voice that what had happened wasn't good and was going to affect everybody.

"Sure as shootin'," his dad said, "We're in it now!"

War had come to the Thomas family that Sunday as it had to millions of other families across America. Michael wanted to get involved right away. The next day he talked it over with his parents, received their blessing and then hitched a ride with his Uncle Jim to the nearest Navy recruiting office. His family was poor, and with two younger brothers and one sister, his leaving home would help relieve the food problem. Many families were still living on the edge of the Great Depression.

But Michael had a secret he hoped the Navy wouldn't discover. After some tense moments he passed the physical, and when he was told he was now in the United States Navy, he actually threw his hat in the air. Within two weeks he was experiencing his first train ride when he was sent to San Diego, California for boot training.

Following six weeks of basic training, Michael stayed on at the San Diego Navy base and was trained as a gunner. When he finished he was assigned to a destroyer headed for the Pacific. And it would be only a short time before he would see his first action. It would come off the island of Guadalcanal, the same time one of his shipmates became aware of his secret.

Michael was frightened the sailor might reveal his secret. It would surely get him kicked out the Navy. He begged the sailor not to tell, but whether he would expose it or not Michael would never know. Their ship was suddenly rocked with heavy explosions. Salt water began pouring in from all directions. Both sailors scrambled up the ladder and found their ship listing badly and fire spreading over the decks. Michael scrambled into his twenty-millimeter gun tub but found his loader dead. He quickly jammed in a round himself and spotted an enemy plane coming in low through the smoke. He opened fire and caught the pilot head-on. He thought it crashed in the ocean behind him. The sound of gunfire and explosions around him were deafening. He began to taste blood in his mouth and his clothes somehow became saturated in hot oil.

The next thing Michael realized was that he was inside a lifeboat lying on his side. He could hear cries for help. With him were only four crewmen, one of them an officer. Their ship had been abandoned, and over the next few hours they helped rescue ten more survivors from the ocean. They watched their burning ship explode some more and then sink. Hundreds would die. Michael had no idea how long he had been in the lifeboat, but as night came they were rescued by another American destroyer. It was then he realized the sailor who had found out about his secret had been killed in the battle.

Michael spent several days on a hospital ship off Guadalcanal before being sent to Hawaii for recovery. He had suffered a wound across his shoulder and left cheek. The officer in Michael's lifeboat boat had told him he had performed heroically at his battle station until he had to be dragged away to abandon ship. He was also cited for helping to save five wounded sailors, including an officer. None of this he remembered doing, except shooting down the Japanese airplane. For this he was awarded the Bronze Star and the Purple Heart. He would later serve on another destroyer in major battles off the Philippines, Iwo Jima and Okinawa.

While waiting at a Navy base on the West Coast in 1944 to be transferred to the East Coast, Michael was sitting on the edge of a lower bunk sharing a magazine with another sailor when through the door of the dormitory came two Navy Shore Patrolmen. Michael caught his breath. He knew they were coming for him. He stood up and waited for them as they approached. They said a few words, Michael nodded, and was then handcuffed. He quietly, but quickly, left the dormitory with the Shore Patrol, got in a car with them and drove away.

Michael served a short time in a Navy brig, was stripped of his medals and then sent home to Kansas City. The Navy had finally discovered his secret.

When Michael Thomas had enlisted he was only 13 years old.

Note: By request, the name of Michael Thomas was used to conceal the true identity of the person depicted in this story.

DOESN'T ANYBODY LISTEN?

While I was researching the little-known and forgotten incidents of the war, I started coming across various incidents that had similarities. It made me stop and think for a minute. It was apparent that during the war an awful lot of people, especially those in authority, just weren't listening, most often because of egos and "What do you know about it?" attitudes. I began to wonder how differently the war might have turned out if they would have just stopped and listened, weighed what they were hearing, then took the time to look into what somebody was trying to tell them before making a decision. Here are just three examples.

Thomas Robert Mackie was a U.S. Navy language officer stationed in Tokyo prior to the United States entering the war. Before the Japanese attacked Pearl Harbor, he was transferred to the Philippines as a member of the CAST crypto code unit. One afternoon, Mackie, who was also an expert on the Chinese language, intercepted a message from the little-known Japanese "Winds" codes. It was in written Chinese characters and stated, in part, the words "east wind rain." Mackie spent hours deciphering the text and became excited when he discovered what those words meant. They were the key to his breaking an almost impossible code.

He gathered up his findings and quickly rushed into his superior's office and laid everything out on his desk. There was no question whatsoever in Mackie's mind about what he had just uncovered. He had decoded the message that read the Japanese were about to attack Pearl Harbor. The officer stared at the papers, then looked up at Mackie. He was told he must be mistaken, but Mackie pointed out to him what certain Chinese characters meant in the coded message. There was no doubt in his mind an attack was about to happen at Pearl Harbor. The officer still didn't believe him, and thought he must be imagining things in those characters. Mackie was ushered out of the office and the rest is history.

Following the D-Day landings in June, 1944, the Allied armies gradually began pushing back the stubborn German forces, but it wasn't coming easily. The enemy's increasingly stiff resistance was becoming a concern among the Allied field commanders. Then a few members of the United States Twelfth Army Group came up with an ingenious idea. They presented it to their commanding officer who said they must be crazy, but he would present the idea to the higher-ups. It was finally approved, mostly because it was just wild enough to work.

It was called Operation Annie. What they did was set up an elaborate underground radio station to operate out of Luxembourg. Their format was definitely pro-German and they totally convinced the Nazis that the broadcast was coming from inside Germany. Many of those broadcasts tricked the German military into giving up well-fortified military positions. Just what the Allies were looking to soften up the German defenses. The deceptive broadcasts played a major role in the Allies final push to victory.

However, it was revealed later that there was one Nazi officer who became suspicious of the broadcasts. He took the matter to his commanding officer who waved him away. The Americans would never think of such a devious plan. One wonders, and I'm sure the suspicious Nazi officer did if he survived the war, how much heavier damage the German army would have afflicted on the Allies if the Nazi command would have listened to the officer's suspicions, and not been deceived into surrendering defenses during a critical time of the war.

Then there was Joseph Stalin. He wasn't going to trust anyone except Hitler, of all people. If he had listened to Winston Churchill, U.S. Intelligence and an Allied spy ring in the spring of 1941, he may have been able to save millions of Russian lives. He was warned that Hitler, who was his ally at the time, was going to unleash a huge invasion force on his country sometime in June. He scoffed at the warnings as being nothing more than British propaganda. And what did the Americans know? They weren't even in the war, although records would reveal later that he was aware at the time that the Japanese were going to strike Pearl Harbor later that year.

On June 22, 1941, the Germans attacked Russia, as warned, across a 1,000 mile wide front. The assault unleashed an awesome army of over three million men spearheaded by 3,000 tanks and 1,800 aircraft. In the first few hours of the attack, Stalin still wouldn't believe what his own intelligence was telling him. He even ordered Soviet antiaircraft guns not to fire on any German planes for fear "it might provoke Hitler." Provoke? When the Russian Premiere came to his senses it was too late. He locked himself up in a room for five days as the German army crushed its way through an unprepared Russia army.

If Stalin had listened to the warnings, the massive Russian army would have been ready and might have stopped the Germans at the border. The tide of the entire war may have been reversed right there instead of four years and millions of lives later.

AN HONORED COWARD

In 1940, as the German army was nearing the outskirts of Paris, a British sergeant major, with the unlikely name of Charles Coward, was captured as his company became surrounded by the swiftly advancing Germans. He was one among the hundreds of British and French troops that were falling in front of the German blitzkrieg that would soon force France to surrender. Coward's capture, however, would be anything but average, to say the least. In fact, he would gain a distinction that no other Allied military person would ever obtain.

After Coward's capture, he was soon marched off to a prisoner-of-war camp in which he wasted little time in finding a way to escape. Under the cover of a moonless night, he slipped away from his captors and within a few minutes had made his way to the outskirts of a small German-held French village. Here he spotted a German night patrol. Hiding in the deep shadow of a doorway, the patrol passed by without him being detected. Suddenly, the German soldiers stopped not more than twenty feet away, lit up cigarettes and began talking. Coward's only escape now was through the door of the building.

After sneaking quietly through the door he found himself in a darkened hallway, which he soon discovered was at the back end of a make-shift German army hospital. Almost on the edge of panic, Coward found himself some hospital patient clothes on a shelf and nervously put them on over his uniform. He then tip-toed his way though another door and into a dark ward where the German wounded lay sleeping. He thought he heard a noise behind him and silently climbed into the first empty bed. How idiotic that was, he thought afterwards. But he didn't know what else to do, and he wasn't going to give himself up. A couple of German patients seemed to take notice of him, but paid little attention, believing that he was no doubt one of them. Exhausted, Coward fell half asleep pondering what to do next.

When daybreak broke, the British sergeant kept himself covered up, but felt certain that any minute he was going to be discovered. He had to get out of there and quick. He slowly climbed out of his bed, and was just starting to shuffle down the aisle toward the back end of the ward from where he had come the night before, when he heard a loud, "Achtung!" He froze as if paralyzed. It was the most frightening call to attention he had ever heard. The German wounded who could stand next to their beds started to do so, while Coward slowly and painfully turned around and stared at a sight that struck even more fear into his heart.

Entering the ward from the other end of the room was a German general followed briskly by an entourage of lower-grade officers. Slowly making his way back to his bed in order not to attract any unnecessary attention, Coward pulled the blanket up under his chin and said a silent prayer. He had no idea he would soon become part of an event that no other Allied serviceman would ever experience.

With perspiration running down his face, Coward lay stiffly in his bed praying the enemy officers would think he was suffering from a fever, and that the doctors wouldn't discover he wasn't one of the patients. Out of the corner of his eye, he noticed the general and his staff moving rather purposely from one bed to the other. He couldn't make out what was going on, but he knew for certain his seconds were numbered.

As the entourage moved next to where he was laying, he closed his eyes and waited for someone to say something he couldn't understand, then drag him roughly out of bed and out the door and onto a truck. Finally he heard a voice that must have been the general's. He spoke a few non-threatening words, tugged lightly on Cowards' shirt, clicked his heels and moved on to another bed. Slowly opening his eyes, Coward looked down at his shirt and what he saw almost stopped his breathing completely. He had just been awarded the German Iron Cross.

Coward must have laid there for what seemed like hours, but in reality were only a few minutes. He couldn't believe what had just happened. Every German soldier in the ward, including himself, had been awarded the Iron Cross for their heroic effort in a recent battle. He thought this just might be his ticket out of there and back to his unit. But it was only wishful thinking. Coward did manage to eventually slip out of the German army hospital, but got only as far the edge of the village where he tried to walk pass an enemy supply truck. It seemed he didn't know as much German as they did, and despite the fact he was wearing his medal, he was quickly apprehended.

Coward would then spend the remainder of the war, five more long years, at a prisoner-of-war camp inside Germany. He may not have been much help to the British on the battlefield, but he at least had the distinction of being the only member of the Allied forces to ever be decorated with the German Iron Cross for Bravery.

Charles Coward's story, however, has an ending that the British major sergeant wanted to be remembered for the most. The German P.O.W. camp he was in was located a short distance from the infamous Auschwitz death camp. During his long stay behind enemy barbed wire, Coward had set up a secret intelligence network that sent information back to the outside free world revealing for the first time the Nazi atrocities taking place at Auschwitz.

This time he wasn't caught.

THE PQ-17

During the very early days of the war, the Russian army was crumbling on all fronts under the pressure of a powerful German offensive. Their survival, and that of their people, depended upon critical war and food supplies getting through to them from the Allies, and the only quick route there was over the icy North Atlantic, through the Barents Sea and into the snow-bound Russian ports of Murmansk and Archangel.

The German strategy to cut this supply line was simple: send out hundreds of submarines and aircraft from occupied Norwegian bases and destroy the convoy ships faster than the Allies could send them. Do this and you bring Russia to her knees and win the war on the continent. But the Allies sent more ships than the Germans could handle, and when the war was over, the price that was paid by the Allies to help save Russia was staggering. To this day, war historians find it hard to believe what the Allies, especially the Americans, sacrificed in these convoy runs to accomplish what was considered to be impossible.

In the summer of 1942, the German submarine U-boats had a strangle hold on the Allied convoys to Russia. Prowling just beneath the surface off the northern coast of Norway, they would ambush the convoys originating out of Scotland and Iceland and send to the bottom one out of every three ships. Those ships that could escape the U-boats would be attacked later by German bombers coming from Norway. In the early going, ships in the convoys were poorly armed and had little or no protection from naval escorts. All this, and the physical torture of constant sub-zero weather and high seas that sometimes capsized ships or cracked their hulls, made the Murmansk run a constant hell.

Out of the literally hundreds of convoys that attempted the treacherous North Atlantic run, one in particular would turn out to be the most catastrophic sea disaster in history. It was known as convoy PQ-17.

On June 24, 1942, a convoy of 33 merchant ships assembled off the coast of Iceland to attempt the ten day, 1500 mile run to Murmansk and Archangel. Out of that total, 22 were American and the rest British, Dutch, Russian and Panamanian. They were to be escorted by more than 40 warships, mostly British. The PQ-17 was to be the most heavily guarded convoy of the war.

Laying undetected off the coast of Norway, ready to strike a death blow to the convoy, was a huge German strike force. It consisted of the German prize battleship *Tirpitz*, several heavy cruisers and destroyers, 25 U-boats and 30 long-range bombers waiting at a base in Norway. As the PQ-17 entered the Barents Sea, British surveillance picked up the location of the enemy task force some distance away and became alarmed that an overwhelming attack on the convoy was eminent. About the same time, the Germans intercepted a British radio signal which led them to believe a trap was being set to destroy the *Tirpitz*. Under a direct order from Hitler, in an effort to save the battleship, the German task force turned around and headed back to Norway. Total confusion on both sides now existed.

Then something so odd happened that it would cause a bitter controversy among Allied leaders and war historians for more than half-a-century.

Not knowing that the German task force had turned back, the British Admiralty, realizing that her lightweight navy escorts would be no match for the awesome fire-power of the *Tirpitz* and her supporting attack units, ordered the escort ships to withdraw from the convoy. The PQ-17 was to disperse and her ships were to scatter in order to fend for themselves. The German's picked up this message and were dumbfounded. Finally deciding it wasn't a British trick, the German naval task force turned around once again and set out to search for the scattering ships. The German bombers in Norway joined in on the hunt and it wasn't long before the complete task force struck unmercifully at the helpless ships.

For three days the relentless German attacks proved to be an unending nightmare for the defenseless merchant ships. Those carrying ammunition and high octane gasoline completely disintegrated from torpedo hits, blowing metal and bodies onto other ships as far away as a mile. U.S. Navy Armed Guard gunners aboard the ships that were still afloat didn't leave their guns for nearly 28 hours; a ceaseless horror of death, fatigue and the hopelessness of manning guns that were almost useless against the enemy onslaught.

Everywhere ships were burning and sinking.

When the attack ceased, the freezing Barents Sea became an escape route for hundreds of merchant seamen and navy gunners clinging to lifeboats and life rafts. Some were picked up by surviving ships while others made it to Norway to be taken prisoner. Many endured as much as two weeks in open boats only to be captured by U-boats, given a little food and water, then set adrift again. And there were those who struggled in the icy water for only a matter of minutes before freezing to death

The disaster of the PQ-17 stunned United States and the British military officials. Its tragic voyage would force convoys to Russia to be suspended for nearly six months. Russian Premier Joseph Stalin accused the Allies of betrayal, and reacted by ordering the bedridden survivors who made it to Murmansk back to Great Britain before they were well enough to leave. And some of those would go down in ships on their return trip.

The result of the attack was unbelievable. Out of the 33 merchant ships, 23 were sunk with 14 of them being American. A staggering 144,000 tons of badly needed war supplies for the Russians went to the bottom. It included 210 fighter planes and bombers, 430 tanks, 3,300 vehicles and millions of gallons of fuel and oil.

The greatest tragedy was the number of casualties. The actual death total, however, has never been accurately counted, but there is belief among some that the toll may have reached over 2,000. It is a known fact that nearly 1,500 survivors were rescued from lifeboats, and many of these were victims of frostbite that would cost fingers, arms and legs. How many survived after being captured by the Germans and taken to prisons in Norway is unknown.

British Prime Minister Winston Churchill called the incident "one of the most melancholy episodes of the whole war."

What really happened during the PQ-17 nightmare is still being debated among historians. Why did the British tell the convoy to split up and run for it because the big German task force was bearing down on them, when it was actually, at the time, heading in the opposite direction due to the German's misunderstanding a British message? Why was it so easy for the Germans to intercept British signals and not vice versa? And yet, the British knew somehow the enemy task force was waiting to pounce on the convoy. To those who survived the attack it didn't matter. As far as they were concerned they were plain abandoned.

Somewhere there's a dusty file in a box stored far away in Great Britain that might give a clue as to why this mysterious order was given for the PQ-17 to scatter. But if the reason hasn't been revealed by now, after more than half-a-century, it isn't likely that it ever will be.

ACE OF ACES

As a boy, I was always captivated by the guy who climbed into the cockpit of a fighter plane, pulled his goggles down over his eyes and flew up and away into combat. I'm sure I wasn't the only kid who felt this way. There was something about a fighter pilot that just made you want to be one. With the war on, many youngsters, when it came to enlist, followed that dream, and went into the air force and got into that cockpit. I decided to go into the navy instead. I couldn't stand heights.

In doing these stories, I decided I would do something about aces. This is the title, as we all know, given to fighter pilots who shoot down a whole lot of enemy aircraft. I never knew how many, so I looked it up. A pilot is considered an ace when he has shot down five enemy planes, and is still considered an ace when he has shot down 20 or 30.

The title of Super-Ace was never given to these pilots, but I imagine it should have been.

I also learned that only one percent of the pilots ever achieved "acedom," yet over forty percent of the enemy planes shot down during WWII were done by aces.

The war produced some outstanding aces. Among the most famous Americans were George "Pappy" Boyington, who downed 28 Japanese aircraft and was awarded the Congressional Medal of Honor. Richard Bong took out 40 enemy planes; Thomas McGuire, 38, and David Campbell, 34. In fact,

Campbell, on October 24, 1944, set a single day American record by shooting down nine enemy aircraft.

Then there was Eric Hartmann. When I stumbled across his record I almost fell out of my chair. What he did you won't find anywhere in the files on American war aces. That's because he fought for the enemy. Despite this, his achievements were mind-blowing, and if they did a movie on him, and passed it off as being true, nobody would ever believe it.

Germany was already embroiled in war when Hartmann became a Luftwaffe fighter pilot in 1941. He was only nineteen and his country's military successes were like a tonic to him. Political hype meant nothing. He only wanted to climb into a cockpit and go fight the enemy in the skies. He was given an ME109, one of the most deadly combat planes ever produced, and on his first mission shot down three British spitfires.

As the war progressed, Hartmann continued to shoot down British planes at such an alarming rate the Royal Air Force put a "bounty" on him. It didn't work. If they ganged up on him he would escape their trap and shoot down one or two of their planes instead. When Europe fell, and the British RAF retired mostly to defend their island country, Hartmann was transferred awhile to the Russian front. It was said he shot down ten Russian aircraft in one day.

The German ace wasn't entirely invincible. In the early going, he was shot down twice over Europe and three times over Russia. Each time he made it back safely to his base.

Then as the United States entered the war, he flew more and more missions and became even more reckless in his tactics. It was rumored he flew combat missions in North Africa, mowing down British and American aircraft like duck pins. He was reported to be everywhere. Over Italy he was the target of an air ambush and was shot down. The Allies celebrated his kill, but within weeks he was sighted again somewhere in the skies over southern France downing an American bomber.

By early 1943, Hartmann had flown nearly 900 missions, shot down over 200 Allied planes and had been shot down himself nine times. Maybe he was invincible. He became known as the Blond Knight of Germany and was hailed as that country's number one hero. He was awarded every medal Germany had, including the Knight's Cross with oak leaves, swords, and diamonds. They didn't get any higher than that in Germany.

As American and Great Britain forces pushed their way up through Italy, and the Russians were driving German troops away from their borders, Hartmann kept up his furious pace in the air. The Allies landed in Normandy, and the handwriting was on the wall. Germany soon surrendered. But not until the Blond Knight had racked up an incredible total of 352 downed enemy aircraft, flew 1,425 missions, and fought in 800 air combats. And believe it or not, he was shot down sixteen times and walked away from each one.

Following the German surrender, Hartmann was taken prisoner by the Americans and given to the Russians where he was sentenced to ten years in prison. After returning to Germany in 1955, the ace of all aces blended into the masses and disappeared. He was reported to have never flown an airplane again.

DOUBLE TROUBLE

In early 1944, the Allies were gearing up for the invasion of Europe. The Germans were sure the jumping off point would be from England, but when and where it would happen they weren't certain. Allied military leaders were getting nervous that the enemy already knew too much as it was. Several diversion tactics had been purposely leaked to German intelligence, but they were still not confident the Nazis were taking the bait. Then screen actor Colonel David Niven stepped forward.

The Allies had already settled on the plan they were going to hit Normandy from England, but in order to take as much pressure as possible off the huge invasion force assembling in England, they wanted to make the Germans believe the D-Day strike was going to be in southern France, and that the build-up in England was only a diversion. The idea was to have British Field Marshall Bernard Montgomery "be seen" by German spies in Gibraltar, which would be a tip-off the Allies were up to something big in that area.

To make the Germans believe that, Niven suggested they use British actor E. Clifton-James, who was a dead-ringer for Montgomery, to serve as a double for the Field Marshall and go in his place to Gibraltar. When Clifton-James, who was already serving as a lieutenant in the British Army Pay Corps, stepped into a room dressed as Montgomery everyone present snapped to attention. Even the real Montgomery's staff members were fooled. The likeness was uncanny. Churchill marveled at the resemblance and Niven was hailed as a genius. But they hadn't delivered their decoy Field Marshall to Gibraltar yet.

Under a blanket of secrecy, Clifton-James and a variety of military personnel were whisked aboard a British transport plane and sent off out over the Atlantic for Gibraltar. Flanked by a fighter escort, the transport stayed far enough off the west coast of France and at an altitude that wouldn't attract trouble from the Luftwaffe. Trouble they got, but not from enemy aircraft.

Clifton-James knew he was about to play the role of his life. He celebrated the fact by toasting his good fortune with the free liquor being supplied by his special staff of officers assigned to the charade. The former actor must have done one too many "God save the King" toasts, because by the time they were halfway to Gibraltar he was stretched out cold in the aisle. Nobody had told the British authorities, including Niven, that the Montgomery wannabe had a reputation of being on a first name basis with any bottle of liquor.

With a welcoming party of military officials waiting for his arrival, an event that was purposely structured to deceive German intelligence, those aboard the British transport now had a crisis on their hands almost equal to that of hiding the original D-Day plans from the Germans: a gassed Field Marshall Bernard Montgomery.

Clifton-James was declared a disaster area. Coffee was being poured down him, but it seemed to evaporate as soon at it reached his lips. He was drug up and down the aisle of the aircraft, but nothing seemed to work. They were only a couple hundred miles from touching down on Gibralter, when one of the people aboard the plane came up with a last-ditch plan that was pure brilliance.

Up near the front part of the transport plane was a small window. With a little effort, it was pried open and Clifton-James was pushed up against the wall facing the window with his head jammed into the opening. The freezing blast of air was a violent shock to his body. A dozen or so more of these blasts and Clifton-James was beginning to lose his slur, and realizing that being "high" was actually being in an airplane 10,000 feet above the ground.

When the plane landed in Gibraltar, Clifton-James was able to get off convincingly as Field Marshall Montgomery. He was spirited away in a car, but was visible just long enough for the Nazi spies to get a good look. The reports went back to Berlin and caused the stir the Allies had hoped. To the Germans, with Montgomery's presence in Gibraltar, the D-Day landings may now occur elsewhere, like southern France, rather than at Normandy. The deception seemed to work. But the Allied high command wouldn't leave well enough alone.

Since Clifton-James was able to sober up enough in time to finally play the role of Montgomery flawlessly to the point of faking out the enemy, a decision was made by the impressed staff who accompanied the actor that maybe he should be seen at least a couple of more times for good measure. And he was sternly instructed to stay away from the booze. He agreed, and a staged social gathering was arranged. The Allies knew that a certain dignitary, a known secret Nazi agent, would be there. He was, and was seen secretly photographing Montgomery. They knew the agent would in turn relay this added proof of the Field Marshall's presence there back to Berlin. The plan couldn't have worked better.

But when German intelligence developed the photos the jig was up. In them, Montgomery was seen smoking a cigar, and even the Germans knew the real Montgomery never smoked and was known to publicly speak out against the habit.

Clifton-James was sent quietly, and unnoticed, back to England without a fighter escort. Here he resumed his mundane desk job in the pay corps. He may have botched up the acting role of his career, but then what chance did he really have in the first place when the charade was titled "Operation Hambone."

EAGLES AND TIGERS

Before the United States entered World War II, there was a group of American men who volunteered to go overseas and fight for the British against the Germans, and for the Chinese against the Japanese. They were all devil-may-care pilots who felt it was a great adventure to do their part to help fight the forces of tyranny, which were beginning to spread across the world. Most of them felt, why not get in on the action now since it was only a question of time before the United States would soon be involved?

They were called the Eagle Squadrons and the Flying Tigers. You probably, no doubt, have heard of these two groups of volunteer air men, but perhaps not some of the details.

In 1940, shortly after Great Britain got into the war against Germany, thirty-four Americans made their way across the Atlantic and volunteered to sign up to fly with the British Royal Air Force. They were an assortment of men whose flying experiences consisted of piloting airliners, crop dusting, doing air-acrobatics in a flying circus, and flying around for fun on weekends. The British welcomed them, but with a rather curious eye.

To accommodate the Americans, the RAF made up a special unit for them called the Eagle Squadron, to be headed by a typical soldier-of-fortune pilot by the name of Colonel Charles Sweeney. This original group became No. 71 Squadron. But British concerns about the Americans soon vanished when on the squadron's first mission they hit a German supply train and destroyed two enemy aircraft. It wasn't long before more Americans arrived, and Squadrons No. 121 and No.123 were added.

In their short tenure with the RAF, before the United States was brought into the war, the Eagle Squadrons had shot down an impressive seventy German aircraft. Then immediately following the Japanese attack at Pearl Harbor on December 7, 1941, the American pilots left the Eagle Squadrons and became the U.S. Army Air Force 4th Fighter Group. When this occurred, only four members of the original thirty-four American Eagle Squadron volunteer pilots were left.

In the Far East, the only mercenary air force in the war was comprised of civilian pilots hired by the Chinese government to shoot down Japanese planes — the famous Flying Tigers. Based in southern China, the American Volunteer Group was led by U.S. Major General Claire Chennault, who was serving as an adviser to Chiang Kai-shek. His pilots were given early P-40 combat planes that were originally built for Sweden, and then turned down by the R.A.F. as being too slow and out-of-date.

With a fierce shark's mouth painted on the nose of each plane, and each pilot trained in Chennault's radical hit and run combat tactics, the Flying Tigers wreaked havoc with their "obsolete" P-40s, and destroyed a great deal of the Japanese air force and their bases in south China. When the United States declared war, the Flying Tigers were activated as the Fourteenth Army Air Force.

Contrary to popular belief, which was stimulated by movies, television and fiction stories, the Flying Tigers original mercenary air force was only in action against the Japanese from

October 24, 1941 until December 7, 1941: a total of forty-eight days. And in that short period of time, the American volunteers, with less than 100 planes, shot down an incredible 286 Japanese aircraft.

One of the most curious rumors that came out of the war revolving around the Flying Tigers was the one about Chennault. In the time before the U.S. came into the war, it was said that Chennault himself had shot down forty Japanese planes. It was never proved, yet there were some of those who were there at the time who claimed he did. If so, then this would have made Major General Claire Chennault one of America's top-scoring combat aces of World War II.

THE RETURN OF THE LONE EAGLE

Marine Second Lieutenant Walter Larsen strapped himself into the cockpit of his gull-winged Corsair fighter plane and was in the early stages of warming up the engine when he received a radio message from the flight tower to move into position on the runway. It was a hot and sticky day. But then all days were like that on Emirau Island. He was to fly to Green Island, approximately two hours away, where he would be assigned to fly fighter escort for military transports.

Larsen taxied his aircraft onto the runway and then turned it to face the full length of the air strip to await clearance for take off. Another pilot was to have flown as his wing man that day, but his plane had developed a brake problem, so Larsen was ordered to go it alone. Then over his head-set came the command, "Hold your position. You're going to have a wing-man."

"Who is it?" Larsen asked.

"None of your business," the tower answered.

Walt Larsen was on his third tour of combat against the Japanese in the South Pacific and he understood people's attitudes were bound to be a little testy if you had spent any amount of time on Emirau — or any of those South Pacific islands, for that matter. The Japanese were always breathing down your back somewhere. He thought nothing more about the curt reply and waited patiently for his wing-man to show up.

A few moments later, Larsen looked to his left and saw another Corsair moving slowly up beside him. Hoping maybe to see one of his squadron buddies filling in the vacancy, he took a long hard look to see who it was. His jaw dropped. He couldn't believe what he was seeing. There was no mistaking who that face belonged to.

Walt Larsen's wing-man was going to be none other than Charles Lindbergh.

To every American, Lindbergh was a bigger than life figure. His daring solo flight across the Atlantic Ocean in 1927 in his single-engine "Spirit of St. Louis" would make him one of this country's, if not the world's, greatest heroes of the twentieth century. His feat earned him one of the largest ticker-tape parades in New York history. But with his celebrity status also came personal pain. The kidnapping and murder of his young son brought world-wide attention and the "Lone Eagle" was again embraced by everyone.

But Lindbergh's friendship in the 1930s with Nazi Germany, because of his interest in aviation, turned off a great many Americans. He also advocated U.S. isolationism while Germany was overrunning Europe. Despite all this, Lindbergh was still the boyish-looking kid next door who had gone where no one had gone before. The nation still loved him.

Following the attack on Pearl Harbor, Lindbergh changed his thinking on isolationism.

Too old to enlist, he went to work for the United Aircraft Corporation and became a technical adviser to the U.S. Army Air Force. Up to this point, his personal life and career is well-

This Marine fighter pilot almost fainted when he discovered who his last minute wing-man was going to be.

known. What isn't known is his unpublicized World War II career. A fact that most Americans had no idea ever existed.

Walt Larsen tapped his helmet with his finger and pointed to Lindbergh to take the lead.

But Lindbergh smiled, tapped his helmet and pointed back to Larsen. What an honor, Larsen thought to himself. They then took off in order and flew the more than five hundred miles together to Green Island without incident. During the flight, Larsen had to shake his head in disbelief that his wing man was none other than Charles Lindbergh.

After arriving at the air base on Green Island, Larsen and Lindbergh joined some other pilots and talked shop about the war and various types of aircraft. The talk lasted for about two hours, and those in attendance were quite taken by this knowledgeable, somewhat shy man, who took a risk back in 1927 that not many in that room would have dared to take.

When Larsen told me this story, I became even more intrigued with Lindbergh. What was this forty-five year old civilian doing flying fighter planes around the South Pacific? I dug through various record books and this is what I came up with. I'm sure this is little-known, if known at all, by the American public.

While working with the Army Air Force, and teaching pilots the various techniques of conserving fuel for long flights, Lindbergh was able to wrangle his way into flying over fifty missions against the Japanese in the Pacific. Since he wasn't in the Air Force, it isn't quite clear, even to this day, how he managed to pull this off. Nobody in the Air Force at the time seemed to have an answer, or particularly wanted to talk about it. I gathered it had something to do about being against the "rules" for having a civilian fly a fighter plane during combat.

But while the authorities were "looking the other way," Lindbergh went about shooting down three enemy aircraft, including one when he took a P-38 up for a routine check-out. There are not many who know this about Lindbergh, and being the kind of man he was, he probably didn't care much if anyone did.

THE LITTLE PRINCESS

One of the most interesting, and somewhat mysterious people to come out of the war was a pretty little Indian Princess by the name of Noor Inayat Khan.

The story goes that she walked into British Intelligence one day and told the first person she saw that she wanted to volunteer her services to fight against Nazi Germany. The Army and Navy wouldn't take her and neither would the Royal Air Force, except for secretarial type work which was not what she was looking for. She needed to get involved physically. She told them she would make an excellent secret agent and that she spoke German, French and Russian fluently. Members of British intelligence sat up and took notice of this fiery little patriot.

Born in Russia in 1914 to an Indian royal family diplomat of sorts from Bombay, the little princess's parents sent her to France following World War I for schooling. She excelled in her studies and also found time when she entered her college years to revel in the carefree student life that was prevalent throughout Europe during the 1920s and early 1930s. It was during this time of her life she became aware of the fascism theology that was spreading across the continent, especially about what was happening in Germany. The Nazi party was coming into power and many of her student friends were being caught up in the euphoria of Hitler's "new world order" doctrine. The little Princess could only sense the sinister motive behind this growing movement inside Germany.

One day in a Paris restaurant, she was lunching with a friend who had heard rumors about the Nazi's persecution of Jews in

Germany. At first she didn't want to believe it, but more stories began to circulate, and then it all became too real when the friend, a boy who was Jewish, found out his uncle's business had been burned to the ground in Germany. It was 1935, and the little princess could see war clouds beginning to form over Europe. Two years later, at age 23, she was in Great Britain.

War in Europe became a reality in 1939 when the Germans crushed Poland and then overran the lowland countries on their way to defeat France. It happened all too suddenly.

The little princess grew anxious and her hatred of the Nazis grew. At that point in time England was bracing for a German invasion and it was then she became determined to do her part to help stop the spread of Nazism.

British Intelligence was finally convinced the little princess might be a valuable asset to its spy operations. She excelled in her training and successfully carried out several assignments tracking down German agents inside England. Then in June, 1943, she was ready to tackle her first major assignment: she was to go behind enemy lines in France and work with the French underground.

On a dark windy night, a small airplane took off from southern England and set off across the English Channel toward France. Its occupants were a pilot and a young woman strapped in a parachute that must have weighed more than she did. After a short time in the air, the pilot nodded to her that it was time for her to jump. With a thumbs up she bailed out into the darkness and the airplane circled around and headed back to England. The little princess from India had landed where she wanted to be: behind German lines where she could do the most good in a strike against Nazism.

On the ground, she was met at a designated place by some French partisans. She gave them her code name of "Madeline", and without a word they rolled up her parachute, hid it in some underbrush, and led her down a dark road to a farm house. There she would coordinate her plans with the partisans that would lead to a series of sabotage projects and spying on the German military in the area.

What the little princess didn't know, and what British intelligence already knew, was that her mission was doomed from the start.

A few days after landing in France, the Gestapo converged on the farm house and arrested the French partisans including the little princess. It was said some of them were shot on the spot, but it was learned later that she was taken away by the Gestapo and interrogated in a nearby village. From there she was herded into a box car with others and taken away to be imprisoned at the Dachau concentration camp.

Some who survived the death camp remember the little princess being there. They say she never denied having been a British secret agent, but only regretted she never had a real opportunity to help bring down the dreaded Nazis. Witnesses said she was executed on September 14, 1944.

Following the war, it was revealed that British Intelligence discovered, after breaking the German code, that the French partisan group the little princess had joined had been infiltrated by a

Gestapo agent. This meant the Gestapo knew she was coming because of their plant, and if the British had called off sending her the Gestapo would have suspected the British of reading their code. The British felt it was too late, and they had no choice but to send her to France without letting her know what lay ahead. They had to sacrifice the little princess in order to protect their spy network inside occupied Europe.

If there is any consolation for the little Princess, it would be in the fact that she more than likely saved hundreds of lives, maybe thousands, and probably even helped shorten the war by unknowingly protecting the British's knowledge of the German secret code.

She did more than her part in helping bring down the Nazis.

THE FORGOTTEN CONVOY

One of the most mysterious stories to come out of the war regarding the hundreds of convoys that made those infamous runs to northern Russia to supply that nation with badly needed war supplies occurred during 1943. It was a strange incident that took nearly a year to solve.

In January of that year, a convoy of American merchant ships left Iceland for the treacherous voyage through German U-boat infested waters of the North Atlantic to the Russian ports of Murmansk, Archangel and Molotovsk. Once they reached the Berents Sea on their last leg into these frozen ports, radio contact between the convoy and the Allies went silent. Usually this was a common occurrence since ships in these icy waters were always in danger from the prowling German submarines and radio silence was imperative. But after nearly a week, and still no word from the convoy, concern began to mount in the United States. Ten days went by, then two weeks. Soon it would become months.

The American convoy had simply vanished.

One must first understand the dreary atmosphere endured by these ships and their crews. The U.S. Merchant Marine and Navy Armed Guard gun crews who made these suicide runs to Russia found those bombed-out northern ports unbearably cold, grim and unfriendly. They lay just outside the Arctic Circle, roughly only 1,400 miles from the North Pole. Strict orders were given to the Americans not to trade with the civilians, socialize with their women, or be found drunk. Most

What happened to this Navy gun crew and a convoy of supply ships to Russia? It's a mystery that took nearly a year to solve.

places, such as a heatless hotel and restaurant that served only black bread and vodka, were off limits. American seaman violating those rules were arrested by the Russians and their commanding officers were helpless to aid them. On top of these miserable conditions were the constant German air raids that kept the cities in total ruins, and her people without adequate heat, food and clothing.

In the meantime, unknown to the Allied command in the United States and Great Britain, the missing convoy had docked at Molotovsk and immediately came under attack from German bombers. These raids would become almost a daily occurrence as they unloaded their cargo. Some ships were set ablaze. Fierce winter storms dropped temperatures to as much as 40 degrees below zero as radio contact with outside Allied authorities remained silenced.

Then as the months brought almost continuous daylight, the vessels were kept from leaving Molotovsk due to the shortage of naval escort ships and the lack of darkness as a cover against enemy dive bombers. Running out of food and ammunition put the crews of the land-locked convoy in a perilous and helpless situation.

Back in the United States, family members of both the Merchant Marine and Navy Armed Guard crews had become deeply concerned. The Allied command was puzzled. Four months had elapsed, and still no word on the whereabouts of the convoy. Were all the ships sunk and their crews dead or missing? Nothing in the way of news was coming out of the Russian ports. Even the German radio made no mention of sinking a complete Allied convoy.

In Molotovsk, navy gun crews aboard these docked ships were still fighting off day and night air attacks from the Germans. Some gunners stayed at their posts continuously. One survivor later tells how he had counted up to 160 daily air raids before he lost interest in counting. During the occasional lulls in the attacks, crews struggled to find something to occupy themselves and get their minds off their near hopeless situation. One tells about rolling up a small wad of rags and taping it together to make a ball so they could play baseball on the deck. When that became boring, they played cards, fought among themselves and wrote letters home that they knew would probably never get there. Some even went ashore and took in the town's only movie theater, only to find it didn't have seats. They had been ripped out by civilians for firewood. Everybody had to stand up and huddle together in order to keep warm. Not exactly the Paramount.

After eight long unbearable months of severe weather, the near exhaustion of men and supplies, and the relentless enemy bombings, the remaining ships of the convoy finally escaped the unforgiving clutches of Molotovsk. By December 1943, they had limped back into New York, the harbor they had left over eleven months before. Not knowing what had happened to the convoy, the missing ships had been written off as having been sunk by the U-boats with all hands either killed or taken prisoner. In fact, the door had been so tightly closed on the matter, that some families had already held memorial services for their loved ones who had been in the convoy.

The U.S. Merchant Marine and U.S. Navy Armed Guard refer to these ships as the "Forgotten Convoy of World War II."

THANK YOU PRESIDENT JAMES MONROE

One of the sea routes the Allies used to send vital war supplies to Russia, other than over the North Atlantic, was through the Persian Gulf and into the various seaports in that region. Russian truck convoys would then come down from the north, load up the supplies and head back up into southern Russia. The route, however, took much longer for the supplies to reach their destination than it did over the shorter, but more dangerous North Atlantic. At a time when ships were being sunk at an alarming rate over the northern route, the Allies decided to concentrate more on the longer but safer Persian Gulf route.

Norman Langelier and Chuck Graycyk, two U.S. Navy gunners aboard a Liberty Ship loaded down with war materials heading for the Persian Gulf, had just survived a murderous convoy run over the North Atlantic and were looking forward to this much warmer and more hospitable climate. After pulling into one of the Persian ports, the merchant marine crews and a local civilian work force begun unloading the ship and stacking the supplies on the dock to await the arrival of a Russian convoy. This usually took a few days, and it would provide those who didn't participate in the unloading, such as the Navy Armed Guard gun crews, some free time for themselves before the ship would pull anchor and head back to the states.

Both Langelier and Graycyk took good advantage of this time away from their ship by shopping the local open-air market. They couldn't believe the beautifully hand-crafted silver jewelry they saw. Both had each picked out an item they wanted, but it was Langelier who became the most excited about a particular silver bracelet. He wanted to take it home to his mother in the worst way.

Before we proceed, keep in mind that this is the same sailor who brought that "priceless fur" home to his mother from Russia.

Not having enough money to make the purchase, Langelier turned to his friend, Graycyk, who informed him he was also broke, but he did have a brilliant idea on what they could trade for these precious items. Langelier quickly reminded his friend that they had been warned by the captain of their ship that it was against the law there for outsiders to do any trading whatsoever with the local merchants. They usually threw you in jail. Graycyk told him not to worry; that the Arabian merchants would be happy to trade with them, as long as the local police didn't catch them. This worried Langelier, but he desperately wanted that bracelet for his mother. So, he reluctantly agreed to go along with Graycyk's idea.

Graycyk's plan was to trade something to the Arabians that they really needed, and that was sheets. He had seen enough movies to know they all wore sheets, and that was what Graycyk and Langelier could get their hands on the most. So they swiped them from their ship. But smuggling the sheets off the vessel was a different matter. They then came up with the idea of wrapping and tying the sheets tightly around their bodies and then putting their clothes on over the top of them. Looking like a couple of over stuffed penguins, they waddled down the gangway and away from the ship without raising any suspicions. Getting away with that alone has to be one of the mysteries of World War II.

When they reached the road leading to the market areas, they suddenly encountered a huge Russian convoy of trucks heading toward them in the direction of the harbor. Preceding the trucks was a military convertible staff car occupied by a high-ranking Russian officer, flanked on each side by soldiers carrying automatic weapons. Among this group was a contingent of fierce looking Gurkers from India, who were night fighters and part of the English fighting forces in the region. The Gurkers wore tall black hats and carried long fierce looking knives.

As the two American sailors tried to waddle pass the oncoming convoy without looking too conspicuous, Langelier suddenly felt a heavy hand come from behind and grip his left shoulder. He was stopped dead in his tracks. As he slowly, and quite painfully, looked back over his shoulder he locked eyes with the biggest and most ferocious looking Gurker one could imagine.

At that moment, Graycyk broke into a run while Langelier stood paralyzed in the grip of his worst nightmare. Then with a sudden jerk, he shook loose and took off after his friend who already had a good ten yards head start. Graycyk's experience as a college football running back, despite all those sheets stuffed under his clothes, gave him an edge as he raced down over a ditch and quickly escaped among some buildings. Langelier only got as far as the ditch when he heard a loud command to halt. Then he heard that dreadful cocking sound of a rifle. Needless to say, he froze.

Langelier was instantly seized by two Gurkers, who both suspected something suspicious was going on when the sheets started to slip beneath his shirt and onto the ground. Despite a few desperate, but rather feeble, protests the sailor was drug away and turned over to the local Arabian police. Before he could grasp what was happening he was shackled in irons and thrown onto the dirt floor of a stockade. Great! Hadn't he told Graycyk it was against the law to trade with the locals?

"I'm an American," he thought. "They can't do this to me." But there he was in irons and nobody knew where to find him. Hours went by and all he could think about was that he was never going to get out of that dreadful place alive. His ship would soon leave without him. Panic really began to set in when later that evening he was given bread and water.

Meanwhile, Graycyk had made his way back to their ship and told the gunnery officer what had happened. This was a serious problem, because the Arabian police usually threw the key away when they locked people up, especially foreigners. The prospects of freeing Langelier looked dim. Then the officer came up with an idea that might just get the navy gunner released. It was a long shot, but probably just crazy enough to work.

The gunnery officer went to the Arabian stockade and pleaded Langelier's case. First he told them they had no authority to hold Langelier because he was an American. That didn't work, so he took a deep breath, crossed his fingers, and went with his plan. He said they could try him, but since he was an American sailor it had to be done aboard an American ship before American authorities. Now who would fall for that? They did.

Still shackled in irons, Langelier was led back to the ship and up the gangway and told quietly by the gunnery officer to get his you-know-what to his quarters in a hurry and stay there. While this was happening, the officer turned to the two Arabian police officers who had escorted their prisoner back to the ship and showed them a book he was holding in his hand.

"I want to inform you," he said, "I have here the Monroe Doctrine, where it says no member of a foreign nation can come aboard a United States ship and take away an American citizen without their consent. In doing so, it could constitute an unfriendly act and lead to war with the United States."

Well, that's not exactly the way it goes, and anyway it has something to do with the Western Hemisphere. But to the amazement of the gunnery officer, who really didn't have a clue what it really said, the Arabian police officers began to back off. They realized they probably had been conned into getting Langelier back on the ship, but apparently they didn't want to mess with the "Monroe Doctrine." They reluctantly left the ship.

The gunnery officer, Graycyk and the rest of the ship's crew all whistled a sigh of relief, while Langelier, still in irons, lay on his bunk in a state of nervous exhaustion. Once his irons were taken off, and in fear they might come back and get him, he never left his quarters until the ship pulled anchor the next day and headed out to sea.

What saved Langelier from probably a lifetime in a dreaded Arabian stockade was pure genius on the part of the gunnery officer. Or maybe it was just plain dumb luck. In any case, it is the only known incident that the Monroe Doctrine was ever successfully enforced by a naval officer who didn't know diddly-squat about what he was doing.

TOO MANY MISSIONS

The name Kurt Hermann is more than likely never mentioned, or recognized, when war historians speak about the great and unsung U.S. heroes of World War II. But to those with whom he crossed paths during his many ventures throughout the conflict he was considered to be some sort of legend. Never seeking the limelight, he seemed to appear here and then suddenly there. There was never anybody quite like Kurt Hermann.

When the war broke out for the United States, Hermann began his participation by joining the Merchant Marine. It wasn't long before the cargo ship he was on was attacked by a German submarine, sending it to the bottom with a staggering loss of life. Hermann was able to jump clear of the burning ship and climb aboard an empty life raft. Here he spent twenty-six days alone on a rolling sea until he was picked up half dead by an Allied ship. This would have been enough war for anyone else, but not for Kurt Hermann.

After being nourished back to health, Hermann enlisted in the Army Air Force. Following his training as a gunner, he was shipped off to North Africa and assigned to the Twelfth Air Force. In his first action as a waist gunner on a B-17 he shot down a German fighter plane, and then added three more kills on his first time out when they moved him over to a B-26. As he kept adding more and more downed aircraft to his record he was soon looked upon in awe by his crews and other members of the Air Force in that theater of war.

In the very first U.S. raid over Rome, Hermann was there fending off German and Italian fighter aircraft as they approached their targets. He would ultimately wind up flying fifty missions before he was forced to take a furlough. But that only made him uneasy, and he longed to get back into action, especially somewhere different. So he sent his request personally to General "Hap" Arnold, stating that he wanted to join the Eighth Air Force stationed in Great Britain. Quite a brave "over-your-head" move for a technical sergeant, but it worked. General Arnold personally saw to it that Hermann was sent to England.

On his first mission over Europe he shot down four German planes. More bomb runs occurred and more enemy planes fell from the skies. His uncanny marksmanship was the talk of the Eighth Air Force. Hermann completed twenty-five missions over Europe, not including the several flights he made as an observer on British bombers. It was never explained how he made that happen.

On one of the missions from England he came down with a cold and was ordered to stay behind. His bomber never came back. Crews wanted Hermann aboard their aircraft as a good luck charm. When the war ended in Europe he sent another request to be transferred to the unfinished business in the Pacific. It was granted and he was immediately assigned to a B-29 group based on Saipan.

After touching down one evening after a raid over Tokyo, Hermann's crew assembled in the mess hall and relaxed over coffee. It was said Hermann was reminiscing about his record and couldn't believe he had just completed his 108th mission. (It was later discovered that he was the first American to accomplish this feat.) He said he had been told soon after transferring to the Pacific that he was the first person to take part in raids on the enemy capitals of Rome, Berlin and Tokyo. When asked how many aircraft he had shot down, his answer was that he never kept count. There are some who flew with Hermann that claimed nobody could have matched his record. Being a waist gunner was his passion.

Upon hearing about Hermann's achievements, the commanding officer of the B-29 unit told the young gunner he should take some time off. There was talk about sending him back to the states for a U.S. Bond drive. Hermann refused and requested that he be able to stay with his crew. Reluctantly, his wish was granted, but for only one more mission, because the U.S. should see what a hero they had in this young man.

One day later, Hermann's B-29 took off for another bombing mission over Tokyo. Only this time it failed to return. No other returning pilots from the mission remember seeing what happened. Hermann's B-29 was never found and the crew was listed as missing in action. Someone had said Hermann was a little edgy before take-off that day, making the comment that perhaps his 108th mission might have been one too many and maybe he should have gone home when he had the chance.

One week later the Atom bombs were dropped on Japan and the war was over.

THE ROLE OF A LIFETIME

The greatest romantic swashbuckler of the silent movie era was none other than Douglas Fairbanks. As one of the Three Musketeers, he would draw his sword and take on a dozen bad guys at one time, swing across the room on a chandelier, do a flip and grab the pretty damsel in distress, run his blade through one or two meanies, and be kissing the young maiden as they swung together on a curtain through an open window.

What a guy! For a dime, kids would catch Fairbanks at a Saturday matinee, then quickly ride their bikes home, and play until dark in an apple tree wielding wooden swords pretending to be their idol. He was the silent movies' greatest hero, not only to kids but to the ladies as well. His heroic achievements on the silver screen are still remembered. There would be nobody, ever, like the brave and fearless Douglas Fairbanks.

Unless it was his son, Douglas Fairbanks, Jr.

Having to grow up in the shadow of his famous father must have been a little difficult for Douglas, Jr. In 1928, he joined the U.S. Navy and served aboard three cruisers before being discharged a few years later. Blessed with the same handsome good looks as his father, he broke into the movies himself in the thirties mostly, some thought, because of his father's reputation. He was first cast in silly romantic roles until he got a big break in 1939 in *Gunga Din*. It was a blockbuster hit, and so was junior. The audience saw a lot of Doug senior in him, and before long he was playing the same type of roles that made his father famous. By the time the war broke out he was established as one of Hollywood's top leading men. However, he still wasn't the huge movie idol and hero his father had been back in the twenties. But he would soon make his mark in another type of theater: World War II.

With the outbreak of the war, young Fairbanks enlisted again in the navy as a lieutenant, and because of his prior naval experience, he was assigned overseas to Lord Louis Mountbatten's Combined Operations Staff. Here he was put behind a desk to work on intelligence projects where he became successful in developing secret plans designed to confuse the Germans. He also helped devise several British commando raids. Most people, especially with his type of background, may have been content to stay behind the desk and out of harm's way. But not Fairbanks. He requested to be up front and in the thick of battle.

His first assignment came in September of 1942 when he led a successful commando raid on a German-held lighthouse on the coast of France. Later, he was in charge of a desert assault on a strategic German outpost in North Africa. Just like in the movies, but only this was for real. He followed this up by taking only four commandos with him as they conducted a raid on the island of Ventotene off the coast of Sicily to capture an enemy radar station.

Elevated to lieutenant commander, Fairbanks helped plan and command a diversion tactic to make the Germans believe an Allied attack across the channel was about to happen.

He led a detachment of PT boats one night toward the French coast and successfully confused the German radar into thinking that a landing force was heading in their direction. The trickery prompted the Germans to pull troops from one area and deploy them in another.

When the fighting ended, Douglas Fairbanks, Jr. went back to Hollywood and resumed his career in the movies. He never talked much about what he did in the war. Those who were under close fire seldom did. He never quite achieved the movie fame his father did, nor did he win an Oscar.

But he did win the Silver Star medal, the British Distinguished Service Cross, and the French *Croix de Guerre*. And you don't earn those on a movie set swinging on a chandelier, grabbing a damsel in distress and flying out a fake window to escape the bad guys.

OOPS!

War historians will tell you that Germany, and Hitler and Goering in particular, made some pretty big boo-boos during the war that sometimes defied common sense. These were caused, most likely, by the arrogant over-confidence that was much the style of the Nazi regime in those days. It's no wonder the Nazi rule only lasted twelve years, and not the one-thousand years Hitler had predicted. A couple of the major mistakes they made are well documented, but worth reviewing. Then there are the goofs you probably never heard about.

In 1940, Hitler had England trapped on their island and on the brink of certain defeat. He could have almost walked across the channel with an invasion force. But Goering talked Hitler into letting his "superior" air force bring the British to their knees with ceaseless bombing attacks. He convinced him that the battered British would surely surrender, and not one German soldier would have to invade English soil to conquer them. Hitler bought into this bravado, and while Goering's air force was conducting its never-ending air raids on the British Isles, the Nazi dictator turned his attention to double-crossing his ally Joseph Stalin by sending his seemingly invincible army into Russia. Didn't he ever read about Napoleon? You talk about things backfiring. The Russian winters strangled the German army into retreat, and Goering's prize air force was being taken to the cleaners by the RAF. The British Isles were saved, and Russia had slammed the door on Hitler.

Thanks, in part, to Herman Goering.

There were other disastrous miscalculations. Like Hitler not listening to his field commanders when Allied forces landed at Normandy. He believed it to be a diversion tactic, and that the main invasion forces would come ashore farther north. Consequently, he held back a whole German division until it was too late. Doing away with Field Marshal Erwin Rommel, recognized as one of the finest military commanders in history, was certainly a brain-dead decision when he was needed the most near the end of the war to defend the fatherland.

It was also the little-known goofs that proved costly.

A few years before World War II broke out in 1939, Germany had developed what they thought was the finest fighter plane ever built. The ME 109, otherwise know as the Mesherschmidt. They also had on the drawing board at the time the HE100, known as the Heinkel fighter, which the developers were excited about because this plane had the capabilities of out performing the ME109. But Goering, who was big man over the German Air Force, preferred the ME 109, because it was already produced and had tested much to his satisfaction. The ME109 was going to be Germany's number one fighter plane, and that was that.

The designers of the HE100, nevertheless, pressed on. They wanted to prove the Heinkel aircraft could do what they said it could. A plane was built and tested, and the results astounded even the designers. The aircraft could fly thirty knots faster than the ME109, was more accurate in getting off more rounds of ammunition, and was able to pull out of a dive much quicker. But for some strange reason, Goering wasn't impressed. He was going to stick with the slower and less accurate ME109.

Russia, in the meantime, heard about the HE100 and purchased six prototypes. They copied them, and consequently the Russian air force became stronger. Ironically, the copies of the HE100 would be one of the deciding factors in turning back the invading Germans a few years later. Chalk up another one for Herman.

When the war finally did break out in 1939, the Germans had produced only twelve of these fighter planes. Strangely, they never flew in combat, but were used only for propaganda purposes. Goering had them photographed many times in different locations and repainted each time to give Allied intelligence the idea they had hundreds of the HE100 fighter planes stationed everywhere and ready to go. It worked, but nobody, to this day, can figure out why Goering refused to build them.

Then there was Hitler's naval mistake. Putting all his chips on the army and air force, he neglected his navy because he felt they weren't as important in his plan to conquer the world. The exceptions, of course, were the submarine U-boats that raised havoc with Allied supply convoys. They were a menacing presence in the early years of the war, but they would lose much of their effectiveness by mid-1943. His three main battleships were lost early, and what other warships were left had little effect on the Allies.

Why Hitler had little confidence in surface warships isn't known. When war historians look at Germany's role in WWII, they become a little mystified by one aspect of naval warfare that Hitler totally ignored, but what proved enormously successful for the Allies: the aircraft carrier.

The Graf Zeppelin was the name of Germany's only aircraft carrier during the war. It was launched before the conflict in 1938, never left the shipyard, and was still under construction when the war ended.

ROCHEFORT TO THE RESCUE

The Japanese attack on Pearl Harbor on December 7, 1941, left the United States Pacific fleet in shambles. Exactly what the Japanese had in mind. This left them able to move swiftly into over-running Southeast Asia without the U.S. interfering. Japan held the winning hand and it would only be a question of time before they would completely dominate that part of the world.

But they had one more task to finish before they could be sure the Americans would not get in the way: seek out the American aircraft carriers that were not at Pearl Harbor and destroy them. The Japanese admiralty figured this would be no problem since their overwhelming superiority in warships would crush the U.S. carriers, which could not expect much in the way of protection from their own Navy because it laid mostly in ruins at Pearl Harbor.

The three American aircraft carriers had been out on maneuvers at the time of Pearl Harbor, and as a result, were ordered to move north of Hawaii to protect the base at Midway Island. Accompanying the flat-tops were eight cruisers, fifteen destroyers and no battleships. Their only chance for survival was to lay in wait and surprise the powerful Japanese fleet before they could land invasion forces. But the Americans weren't positive if Midway was the actual intended target. To make sure, they turned to Admiral Chester Nimitz in Pearl Harbor and his number-one code breaker, U.S. Navy Lieutenant Commander Joseph J. Rochefort.

Rochefort was a genius at deciphering codes. Now he had the task of listening in on the Japanese code that might tell him what their intentions might be. But the Japanese were being careful not to reveal anything specific. Then Rochefort thought of a plan that would, hopefully, draw the Japanese out and reveal what they were up to.

Midway Island was a U.S. Naval base located nearly 1,200 miles west of Hawaii. It was used primarily as a refueling base and airstrip, and was protected by a small military garrison. Rochefort had the garrison send out a message to Pearl Harbor stating they were getting low on drinking water. Japanese Admiral Yamamoto took the bait and radioed his forces about the shortage of water at Midway, thus confirming suspicions that Midway was indeed the Japanese target. The American aircraft carriers and their support ships then placed themselves between Midway and the oncoming powerful Japanese naval strike force. The enemy advantage was overwhelming. They had eight aircraft carriers, eleven battleships, eighteen cruisers and sixty-five destroyers. But hopefully the element of surprise would favor the Americans.

Then on June 4, 1942, before the Japanese could detect anything out of the ordinary, American carrier-based aircraft struck the approaching Japanese head-on. The unexpected first blow stunned the Japanese as the first American wave of aircraft scored direct hits. The Japanese retaliated by sending up planes to battle the surprise intruders, while in the meantime, waves of more American planes zeroed in on the Japanese warships, especially the aircraft carriers; sinking them, or seriously damaging their flight decks, leaving the Japanese planes that were already airborne no base to return to.

The battle for Midway raged for two days with a resounding defeat of the Japanese. The entire battle was fought without an exchange of gunfire from the ships on both sides. It was fought in the air by attacking aircraft, and the cost to the Japanese was devastating.

They lost four aircraft carriers while the U.S. lost one carrier, the *Yorktown.* The U.S. victory was due to its ability to secretly read the Japanese code, thanks to Joseph J. Rochefort.

The Japanese had been stopped short of Midway, and the turning point of the war was established. From June 6, 1942 on the United States moved from being on the defensive to the offensive. It had been Japan's first naval defeat in more than three hundred years.

Rochefort was also responsible for making the Japanese submarine force ineffective throughout the war by deciphering their code. U.S. warships and aircraft most often were able to seek them out and destroy them before they could attack Allied shipping. Admiral Nimitz credited Rochefort for probably being the one single American responsible for starting the turn around in the war that would ultimately favor the United States in the Pacific.

Many military officials and war historians claim that if the Japanese had taken Midway there would have probably been no stopping them in their conquest of Hawaii and then reaching the shores of the United States.

THE GREAT DANE

When the German army rolled through Denmark in 1940, there was one man who wasn't going to back down from the Nazi regime. It was King Christian of Denmark.

Rather than go into exile, or hide behind the walls of his palace for the duration of the war, King Christian chose to stay put and do whatever he could to protect his people from the Nazis. If that meant he had to personally get involved, he would.

During the first days of the German occupation, the King met with the German military and the dreaded Gestapo. One of the first orders he was given was that all Danish Jews had to sew a large Star of David on their clothing. The King knew very well what this identification would mean, having been aware of what the Nazis did to the Jews in Poland, as well as in their own country. He was determined to not let it happen in Denmark.

When the Star of David order was announced on the radio and in the newspapers, King Christian promptly became one of the first to sew the star on all of his clothing. The Nazis were shocked because the King wasn't Jewish. When word spread throughout Copenhagen about what the King had done, the citizenry began doing the same thing. Before long the entire city was wearing the Star of David. Then, much to the growing frustration of the Nazis, everybody in Denmark, including infants, had the Star of David displayed prominently on all their clothes.

Then in 1943, a German shipping official attached to the German legation in Copenhagen, tipped off the King that the

Nazis were getting ready to deport the Danish Jews to concentration camps. King Christian became more determined than ever to do something about this outrage, and when the Gestapo began closing down Jewish stores and breaking down doors to take away whole Jewish families, he felt he had to act immediately. His advisers warned him not to get directly involved in stopping the Germans, or it might cost him his life by "accident." The King reminded them that these people were citizens of Denmark and he had sworn to protect them the best he knew how.

Within the palace walls, away from the shadow of the Nazis, King Christian took it upon himself to draw up a plan to smuggle the Jews out of Denmark. He gathered around him a few of his most trusted aids, met secretly with the Danish Resistance, and with assistance from a close friend in the Swedish embassy, the King set in motion one of the most daring Jewish escape plans of the war.

Right under the noses of the ever-present menace of the Gestapo, the King started evacuating the Danish Jews to Sweden. Some went by sea on fishing boats hiding beneath hundreds of fish, others escaped by night covered up in produce trucks, while still others walked all the way under various disguises, or hid in shipping crates on freight trains; all according to a wide variety of diversion plans intended to keep the Gestapo elsewhere. He was able to save more than 6,000 Jews.

Then one day, King Christian almost pushed his courage a little too far. It's been said that one of his aids, who was with the King at the time, almost fainted from fright.

While motoring through the streets of Copenhagen, the King and his aid passed a building that was flying the German swastika flag. The King ordered his chauffeur to stop the car, whereupon he stepped from the back seat and stood in the middle of the street looking up at the flag. A German officer who was standing at the entrance to the building approached the King and asked him what he was doing.

"I order you take that flag down," the King demanded. "It is in direct violation of the Danish-German agreement of occupation."

The Officer stared at the King, whom he recognized, and curtly told him, in no uncertain terms, it was there by order from Hitler and would remain there.

"If that flag is not down by noon," the King replied, "I will send a soldier to take it down."

"If you do," the officer snapped back, "he will be shot!"

"Then I will be that soldier," the King said, "and will return at noon to take it down personally."

The King climbed back into his car, and with his wide-eyed chauffeur behind the wheel and his perspiring aid sitting next to him, they sped off to the palace. It was already 11:30.

At preciously noon, a nervous chauffeur drove King Christian back to the building.

The German officer was gone and so was the flag.

HERE'S TO MIDNIGHT CHARLIE

During the heat of the war in the South Pacific, a Marine air squadron that had been flying air-strikes out of Henderson Field on Guadalcanal was transferred over to the Piva Yoke airstrip on Bouganville. Their mission was to fly bomber escort and fighter sweeps over the Japanese held Rabaul Harbor and enemy targets on New Britain and New Ireland Islands. You talk about the enemy being on your doorstep at Henderson Field, this place was ridiculous.

The Japanese at the time had control of the entire island, except for a semi-circular area about 6,000 feet long, with the ocean at one end of Torkina Bay near an active volcano. Within the perimeter, there were three airstrips: Piva Yoke with fighter planes; Piva Uncle with torpedo and dive bombers; and Torkina with P-38 night fighters. With the Japanese milling around somewhere just beyond those air strips, you stayed pretty close to the runways.

By day, the defenders of the strips were able to keep the Japanese at bay, but when night came it was a different story. The pilots needed their sleep and it was getting increasingly difficult for them to do so with the enemy's "Midnight Charlie" visits from Rabual. Every midnight, and you could set your watch by it, the Japanese would send over a slow-flying "Betty Bomber" to drop a few 100 pound bombs near the air strip. Their accuracy was a joke, but the loud whistling noise from the dropping bomb, followed by the sound of the explosion, made it almost impossible for the American flyers to get any rest. The enemy tactics were working, and something had to be done about it.

To get even, the Americans started flying their own midnight runs over the Japanese airstrip at Rabual and dropping 100 pound bombs. The effect was the same. But night after night, with both sides dropping these shrieking bombs, it was unnerving. Plus, a lot of ammunition was being used on our side, and soon, at this rate, there would be none left. Then came a bright, typically American, idea.

While a few of the sleepy-eyed pilots were discussing the predicament over some beers in the mess tent one evening, one of them remembered being a kid back home and blowing air across the top of an empty bottle to create a deep whistling sound. So, why wouldn't it make the same sound, he reasoned, if it was dropped from an aircraft and had all that air rushing through it? They all looked at each other. Maybe this guy was a genius. And why wouldn't it get louder and louder the more bottles you bunched together? And look at the 100 pound bombs that would be saved. It was worth a try.

The next day, they secured about two dozen empty beer bottles together and gave them to the bombardier of the B-25 scheduled for that night's run over Rabaul. The result was a resounding success. The loud whistling noise from the bottles was identical to that of dropping a 100 pound bomb. There was no explosion, but it produced the same troublesome effect on the Japanese. From now on, no rest for the wicked.

As the nightly raids continued, more and more beer bottles were added to the drop, and the more that were tied together the louder and more terrifying the whistling became. After only a few nights of this, the Japanese had had enough and gave up their "Midnight Charlie" attacks. In return, the American pilots were finally getting some sleep, their ammunition was being saved for more meaningful missions, and all the empty beer bottles on the base had been recycled.

THE UNKNOWN NAVY

During the war, there was a little-known branch of the United States Navy called the Armed Guard. Most people never heard of them. That is because nobody made an effort after the war to fully record their achievements. Even today, there are some U.S. Navy Department officials who would be hard pressed to remember who they were and what they did.

Yet they had a staggering 710 ships sunk beneath them.

The Armed Guard was a group of sailors who were trained as gunners, signalmen and radiomen to serve aboard merchant ships that delivered essential war supplies to the Allied military forces throughout the world. It wasn't a very glamorous assignment. Not like being on a battleship, an aircraft carrier or a destroyer. They usually had to man outdated World War I guns, especially during the early part of the war that, on occasion, wouldn't even fire. And there were no doctors aboard their ships.

Since the United States was totally unprepared for war when the Japanese pulled their surprise attack on Pearl Harbor, training for those being placed in the Armed Guard as gunners was inadequate, to say the least. There were hardly any deck guns to train with, and at one camp there was only one training gun for every 500 men.

At the beginning of the war, the ships they sailed on were nothing more than old, slow freighters, usually overloaded with planes, tanks, oil and ammunition. In those early days, many sailed without any guns whatsoever. It's a recorded fact that one ship installed wooden telephone poles on deck and painted them gray in an effort to make the German U-boat captains believe that the ship they saw through their periscope was heavily armed and that it might not be wise to attack it.

Living conditions on the early merchant ships were usually deplorable and recreation facilities just didn't exist. Medical assistance was nothing more than a large first aid kit, and in the North Atlantic, where convoys of these ships were running supplies to Russia from Great Britain, their chances of being sunk by a German U-boat, or an enemy bomber, was one in three. In the Pacific, they were the constant target of Japanese suicide planes.

The American merchant seaman had already been involved in the war prior to Pearl Harbor by sailing supply ships under the Lend Lease Act to help Great Britain. They had already experienced the horror of war before the United States entered the conflict.

At first, the merchant seamen resented the young green navy gunners coming aboard their ships. Friction between the two groups grew mostly out of the merchant marine seaman looking down on the Armed Guard as being castoffs from the navy, and the Armed Guard crews viewing the merchant mariners as overpaid drifters. But after both factions began to experience the nightmare together of having their ship torpedoed, seeing their friends die, and facing the stress of being adrift on a life raft, the bond between the two grew to one of mutual friendship and respect.

During those long war years, foreign war correspondents were writing back home about the heroic achievements of our fighting men from all branches of the military. All except the Navy

The S.S. Jeremiah O'Brien *is one of only two WWII Liberty ships afloat today. These "ugly ducklings" did the impossible in helping the allies come back from the brink of disaster to win the war.*

Armed Guard. The Armed Guard had no one on board their ships to report back about what it was like being on the flaming deck of an oil tanker in the Mediterranean, adrift for weeks in a lifeboat in the frozen North Atlantic, captured and bayoneted on the deck of a Japanese submarine in the Indian Ocean, or one of a few survivors of a Japanese suicide airplane attack on a Liberty Ship in the Pacific. There was no Ernie Pyle to sing the praises about these young men; no one to applaud their heroism, sacrifices and devotion to duty. Percentage-wise, their death toll was among the highest of the war.

Nobody in the history of world warfare faced the enemy on more fronts at the same time than did the U.S. Navy Armed Guard during World War II. They wore no special ensigna to distinguish who they were, and while they received a special citation and commendation from the governments of Great Britain, Russia and France, they never received such an honor from their own

country. Almost on the day Japan surrendered to end all hostilities, the Armed Guard was disbanded and the sailors were either reassigned elsewhere in the navy or honorably discharged.

Many of the Armed Guard veterans became a little bitter following the war when their own navy didn't give them the proper recognition, or even admit who they were. One example was when the Armed Guard

These two sailors were part of a U.S. Navy unit that lost more than 700 ships during WWII. Yet hardly anybody, including some in the Navy Department, had ever heard of them.

veterans were planning a reunion in California and telephoned an admiral to ask if he would speak to them at their banquet. The admiral's answer was, "Armed Guard? What the hell is that?"

Then in 1998, after more than fifty years of being forgotten, or ignored, the United States Navy Armed Guard's heroic war record was entered into the Congressional Record. The last military combat force from WWII to receive the honor. It came about only because of the persistence of several Armed Guard veterans who just wouldn't give up.

Each year, the remaining Armed Guard veterans, who are still able, try to attend a national reunion to visit old shipmates. Being a proud member of that special group, I was attending one of those reunions in St. Louis when one of the veterans handed me a piece of paper. Written on it was something that I feel just about sums up the U.S. Navy Armed Guard.

For every soldier or marine that stormed a beachhead, for every air bombardment or enemy aircraft shot down, and for every tank, plane and round of ammunition supplied to our fighting forces and allies, it never would have been accomplished without the United States Navy Armed Guard protecting the ships of the Merchant Marine.

– author unknown

The U.S. Navy Armed Guard motto was "We Delivered!" And they did.

THE PAPERHANGER

When France surrendered to Germany in 1940, Hitler had control of all Europe. Thousands of British forces, through the miracle of Dunkirk, had escaped back to England to await their fate, Spain was a neutral ally, Italy had already sided with Germany, and it was only a matter of time, he thought, before North Africa and the oil-rich nations of the Middle East would be his. His next big target, however, was Russia.

Despite concentrating on Russia, and figuring he could blockade Great Britain into surrendering, Hitler's military advisers recommended that defensive fortifications should be installed along the English Channel opposite the British Isles just in case those pesky Brits felt like coming back. Hitler thought it was nonsense, since the war, for all practical purposes, was already won. Someone next to the German dictator — and history doesn't tell us who — made a convincing point to him about the need for the fortifications. Within a few months, German engineers were given instructions to go ahead with the plans and make it the most impregnable line of defense in the history of warfare. If you're going to do it, you might as well do it right.

Sometime during 1941, several German engineer officers took over a French estate to finish the final work on the plans. The main house was somewhat in need of repair, due to a past battle in the area, so local carpenters, painters and labors were called in to fix the place up. They were told to follow the restoration instructions according to the lieutenant in charge, do a good job, and stay out of the way of the engineers. Among those agreeing to do so was a little man by the name of Rene Duchez, whose specialty, he told the lieutenant, was paper hanging.

Work on the old estate proceeded as planned and most of Duchez's work was completed in two weeks. He suggested to the lieutenant that perhaps the walls of the main room of the house, where the engineers were working, should also be papered. He reluctantly agreed, and Duchez promised the officer he would not get in the way of the engineers. He said they would hardly even know he was there.

As Duchez went about his work, the engineers poured over their plans and paid little attention to the little Frenchman. They should have. While engrossed in their work, Duchez eyed a map on one of the cluttered tables. It seemed to be one of several copies of one particular area. Understanding German, he over-heard that this was the coastal area where they were going to build something called the Atlantic Wall: the defense fortifications in Normandy, no less.

It isn't quite clear how Duchez managed to pull this off, but he was able to, over a course of a couple of days, move that one copy of the map, without being noticed, closer and closer to the wall near the end of one table. Then when the right moment came, when he was left alone for a few minutes in the room during a lunch break, he slipped the map behind a picture on the wall over the table. It was said he practiced this maneuver at night at home to make sure the move would go quickly and smoothly if the opportunity presented its self.

The job on the estate soon ended, and Duchez went back to his home nearby. He wasn't paid for his work. Weeks went by and the German engineers still occupied the house. Then one afternoon they packed up their plans and left the estate. But the house was still occupied by other German officers. Getting that map of the fortifications out from behind that picture was going to be tricky, and certain death if he was caught.

Then one day, Duchez went to the estate to see the lieutenant who had been in charge of the work force during the restoration. He asked the officer if he could check the wallpaper work he had done in the main room because he was worried about one particular spot he didn't think was quite right. The officer first told him to leave the premises, but then for some unexplained reason he called him back to go do what he had to do, but to do it in a hurry.

Duchez walked into the room and found nobody there, but he could hear voices. He went to the picture on the far wall and for a moment stared at it as his heart almost pounded through his shirt. Wait a minute, he thought. What if this was a trap and he was being watched? Had the Germans discovered the hidden map behind the picture? If they saw him look behind the frame it would be a dead giveaway he had put it there. He would surely be taken outside and shot.

Duchez was going to take the chance. He glanced around the room, then slid his hand swiftly and quietly behind the picture, just like he had been practicing. It was there! He pulled it out, slipped it under his shirt and walked casually out of the room and closed the door behind him. He saw the lieutenant coming toward him, and with a wave and a smile he told the officer the finished wallpaper job looked fine and apologized for being such a bother. The officer stopped, shrugged his shoulders and walked away in the opposite direction.

With the help of the French Resistance, the map was successfully smuggled out of Europe and into the hands of the Allied military command in England. They couldn't believe their good fortune. Here they had a map with a detailed outline of the German fortifications that were going to be built along the Normandy coast line. This gift, from a loyal French paperhanger, would come in handy when the Allied forces would invade Normandy three years later in June, 1944.

General Omar Bradley, one of America's greatest four-star generals who wound up commanding four armies during WWII, called Rene Duchez's daring act an "incredible and brilliant feat, so valuable that the D-Day landing operation succeeded with a minimum loss of men and material."

This time the little Frenchman was paid for his work. He was awarded the Bronze Star for Bravery.

THE FLAT TIRE

Donald Chance and Mike Drugan had been close friends when they graduated together from a Chicago high school in the spring of 1940. That summer they decided to motor west in Drugan's 1930 Chevy to find work as carpenters in the movie studios of Hollywood. They figured they couldn't act, so why not break into the movies by working behind the scenes. Maybe a little of the glamour might rub off on them.

Along the way they decided to challenge Colorado's Pike's Peak highway. It was more that 12,000 feet to the summit and there was some doubt expressed by Chance that Drugan's Chevy could make it to the top. Drugan assured his friend there shouldn't be any problem. His little car could overcome any obstacle. So, with blind faith as their passenger and a large coffee can of water setting between them for insurance, they started up the steep incline. After a couple of stops to refresh the radiator, they reached the top without a hiss of steam. They celebrated by eating tuna fish sandwiches.

But on their way back down, one of the tires blew and the car came to a stop on a slight downgrade. In their attempt to change the tire, the tire jack slipped due to the unevenness of the road, pinning Drugan helplessly beneath the car. Chance was unable to lift the vehicle, and due to the late hour, traffic had ceased in both directions. Making his companion as comfortable as possible, Chance started for help by running down the mountain road hoping to get assistance. He couldn't believe there were no cars in sight anywhere. It was now dark, and in a state of near panic, he stopped and decided to run back up the road to be with his friend. Suddenly, headlights pierced the darkness behind him. It was a flat-bed truck.

With the aid of three men in the truck, the Chevy was lifted off Drugan and he was placed on the back of the truck covered with the two boys' sleeping bags. With Chance at his side, the truck raced down the mountainside for medical help. Drugan would recover, but barely. The doctors told Chance and the three people from the truck that if they had been only minutes later in lifting the car off of Drugan it might have been too late for him.

Chance and Drugan never made it to Hollywood. They returned to the Chicago area and worked doing odd jobs while Drugan healed from his ordeal. Then came the attack of Pearl Harbor on December 7, 1941. Within two weeks they both had enlisted in the Army and they would stay together through basic training before being separated. It would be the last time they would meet up with each other again until the fall of 1944.

Donald Chance was shipped overseas and went ashore on the American landing at Casablanca. He fought the Germans through the North Africa campaign, then Sicily and up into Italy. Later, after the Allied D-Day landings at Normandy, Chance was transferred from the Italian war zone up into southern France, then eventually into Belgium following the Battle of the Bulge. All this time he wondered about his friend Mike Drugan.

As the convoy of trucks in which Chance was riding moved slowly north in a heavy downpour through the Belgium country side, they came upon a stalled Jeep blocking the middle of the road. Being in the cab of the first truck of the convoy,

Chance jumped out and ran ahead to see what had happened. Gathered around the rear of the Jeep were three soldiers trying to lift it off someone beneath the left rear tire. With Chance's help they succeeded. And there laying in the mud half-conscious, and delirious, was his friend Mike Drugan.

"He was trying to fix a flat," one of the soldiers said," and it rolled down on him. If you guys hadn't come along in time we wouldn't have been able to save him. He kept mumbling about some guy named Don Chance who had gone for help."

Both Donald Chance and Mike Drugan survived the war. They returned to Chicago, married and raised families, and would see each other occasionally. Then Chance died of a heart attack in 1977.

In the summer of 1979, Drugan and his wife started driving west to visit their only daughter and her family in California. On the way their car had a flat tire. As Drugan removed the tire, the tire-jack slipped and pinned him beneath the axle. Only this time it was fatal. They were just four miles from the entrance to Pike's Peak Highway.

THE VISIT FROM ERIC

Helen Travis graduated from the ninth grade in June, 1943, just three days before her bother John was drafted into the Army. She remembers being at the train station with her mother, father and younger brother when he left. For Helen, it was especially hard because she idolized her brother.

For the past year and a half she had worked for him as his book-keeper for the three produce stands her father let him operate for him in rural Iowa. She was smart in arithmetic and her brother had her keep very simple records in a notebook. This made her feel important and she never knew him to check her adding and subtracting.

But it was the fun times she cherished the most with John; when she would ride in the flatbed truck with him and pick up the produce and deliver it to the stands that were located at various road intersections throughout the county. He was kind, loving and admired by everyone. She felt it was unfair that the Army should take him away. He left on his twenty-first birthday.

Following his basic training, John came home for a week on furlough. There were picnics with family and relatives and a time for being with his girl friend. And he found a special a time for Helen. They visited his produce stands, and laughed over Cokes about the funny things that happened to them while growing up. Especially the day they lost almost half a truck load of corn when John let her drive. He took the blame and told his father he was looking at a couple of girls walking along side the road when he slid into a ditch. Nobody really believed him, so Helen confessed and got him off the hook.

Then he was gone. A star was hung in the window and Helen soon found a job at the local ration board. She joined the Red Cross, gave blood and bought savings bonds. She wrote John a letter once a week, and when he could write he had a special letter in his envelope for her. A year had passed and they became aware by one of his letters that he was now overseas, somewhere in France.

She remembers it was an exceptionally warm day when her folks were notified that John was listed as missing in action. The stunning news seemed like a bad dream. It wasn't as though she never thought about the possibility it would ever happen. But now that it had, she was dazed into disbelief. Her father reminded her that John was reported missing, not killed. This gave Helen and her family a little hope, and they would pray nightly that he would be safe and reappear somewhere. But Helen knew, as well as her parents, that as each day passed with no word on his whereabouts, it was another day closer to realizing he might never come back.

Two months after the news, Helen was returning home one evening after seeing a movie with some friends and was walking up the long walk to her home when she saw someone quietly step out from behind a tree at the edge of the family orchard. It was dark and only the dim light from the front porch light pierced the blackness of the night. She recalls that the sudden movement of the dark figure, for some reason, at first didn't startle her. For an instant she thought it might be her younger brother trying to scare her. But as the figure stepped closer to her she stopped and stared. It was a man and he was wearing a uniform. For one heart-pounding moment she was sure it was John. Then he spoke:

"I hope I didn't frighten you. My name is Eric and you must be Helen. John has told me so much about you."

Helen doesn't remember answering. She was surprised she could hear his voice above the pounding of her heart.

"John wants you to know he's okay," he said. "He's in a prison camp in Germany, has a slight wound just above his left wrist, and for you not to worry. When the war is over he'll come home and everything will be the same again."

He smiled and then turned away and walked back into the shadows of the orchard. Helen stood there for what seemed like forever, never saying a word. She couldn't believe what she had seen and heard. She started to call after him, but instead suddenly started running up the long walk, leaping the steps of the porch and bursting through the front door.

Helen excitedly related to her parents what had happened out in front of the house. Her father went outside with a flashlight and called after the soldier, but there was no response. John was alive, that's all that mattered to Helen, and he would be coming home.

But Helen's father and mother were a little mystified. Who was this soldier named Eric and why didn't he come to the front door and tell them? Why hide in the shadows outside and then just walk away? Maybe it was somebody playing a trick on

Helen because they knew how much John meant to her. Or was she just imagining the soldier because the news he brought about John was something she desperately needed to believe in.

Helen's father checked with the military and there was no evidence that John had been taken prisoner. He was still listed as missing in action. The experience with the mysterious soldier soon faded away and as the months dragged by neither parent spoke about it again.

All except Helen. The encounter had changed her from being depressed and never smiling to a happy young girl full of enthusiasm and a new love for life. She believed the soldier had been there and told her about John.

When the war ended in Europe in May, 1945, American soldiers started coming home.

Helen studied the many photographs that appeared in the newspapers and magazines of those returning, hoping to recognize John among them. Then it happened. In late May they were told John was among those released from a German prisoner-of-war camp. He was alive and would be home soon, just like the soldier said he would. The joy in the Travis home was unexplainable.

Not long after John had returned home, Helen was sitting alone with him on the front porch and began telling him about the incident with the soldier named Eric who told her not to worry because her missing brother was a prisoner of the enemy and would return home safely. John looked puzzled, then explained to Helen he never knew a soldier with a first name of Eric; not in basic training nor in his outfit overseas.

Nearly sixty years have passed now and Helen still believes she was approached that night in front of her house by a soldier named Eric. If he was something she just imagined then how did the soldier know that John had been taken prisoner while the U.S. military had no knowledge of the fact until the war in Europe was over? How do you explain the wound on John's wrist that he knew about? And how did he know Helen's first name?

Helen doesn't really care anymore whether people believe her or not about Eric. The only thing that mattered at the time was that she knew for sure John was alive and would survive the war because Eric came and told her so.

MAN OF WAR

Charles Michael Sweeney couldn't have been more than nine years old when he first day-dreamed about riding into battle and leading a charge against an enemy stronghold. To him, nothing could be more glorious than that. While other boys were out fishing or playing baseball Sweeney was staying home and reading all the books he could find about the recent Civil War. There was no doubt in his mind he was going to be a soldier. Nothing was going to hold him back.

By the time he graduated from high school in 1900, Sweeney was confident and ready to obtain his first goal: to be admitted into West Point. He had been an excellent student and had little trouble in being accepted. But the one thing Sweeney lacked was patience. The Spanish-American War was underway and the temptation to get in on the action was more than he could stand. He dropped out of West Point and joined the regular Army as a private and happily marched off to war.

When the Spanish-American conflict ended rather abruptly, Sweeney was soon discharged and left stranded without a war to fight. Then he remembered that during his adolescent days he had read books about the French Foreign Legion which was always fighting somebody in the North African desert. He wasted little time booking passage on a steamer and within the first day of his arrival in Algiers he signed up with the Legion. Here he distinguished himself as a courageous fighter and soon rose to the rank of captain. But after a few years of desert warfare something even bigger was beginning to loom on his horizon: World War I.

Sweeney resigned from the French Foreign Legion and caught a ship back to the United States to once again join the U.S. Army — only this time as a major. He set sail for France with the first American troops, and when the war ended, he had taken part in all the major battles. He was awarded several combat medals, but they meant nothing to him if there were no more wars to fight. As American troops were returning home for victory parades, Sweeney went in search of areas of unrest. His next stop: Turkey. Here he joined the Turkish Army and quickly became a general.

After a couple years of leading Turkish troops in putting down various rebel uprisings, Sweeney became bored and resigned. It was now the late twenties and Poland was beckoning him with its historic and gallant cavalry. Sensing Europe was about to explode into war, he enlisted in the Polish army and was immediately made a general. But for Sweeney the war clouds were too slow in forming. After a few years of impatience, he once more caught a steamer for Algiers and rejoined the French Foreign Legion. Then civil war erupted in Spain, and our traveling soldier was soon leading Spanish loyalist troops against the rebels.

In the late 1930's, Russia invaded Finland, and seeing that the Spanish Civil War was now history, Sweeney jumped at an opportunity to get involved. He persuaded several American civilian pilots to form a special air force unit that would fight on the side of the Finns. It was beginning to take shape when, to Sweeney's disappointment, the war ended. But the war clouds he had seen forming over Europe for several years were now taking shape. In September, 1939, Germany invaded Poland and the greatest war in history was underway. Sweeney finally had the one big battle he was looking for.

Not waiting for the United States to get involved, which he knew his country would eventually do, Sweeney organized a volunteer group of thirty American pilots and took them to France. They became a special air-combat group for the French Air Force. But Hitler's armies were rolling non-stop through Europe and were fast-approaching Paris. The French were going down in defeat, and Sweeney barely got his American pilots out of France and over to England.

Once in England, Sweeney didn't give up the hope of assembling an all-volunteer American air force. He fell short of getting it organized in Finland, had it operational only for a few weeks before the French surrendered to the Germans, and now he had this golden chance with the British. To make it happen, he joined the Royal Air Force as a colonel and was immediately appointed commander of his American volunteer fighter air group which would become known as the Eagle Squadron. Their short war record for the British, before the United States entered the war, was one of the most impressive of World War II. Then when the U.S. became involved, the Eagle Squadron disbanded and Sweeney, and what was left of his small group of American volunteer pilots, became the U.S. Army Air Force 4th Fighter Group.

As for Charles Michael Sweeney, the war ended in 1945 and so did his incredible military career. The only thing that kept him from joining the Army in 1950 to fight in Korea was his age. The old warrior was 70 years old and still looking to find a battlefield. Nobody in the history of the world had a fighting record that came anywhere near his.

Sweeney died in 1963. He had fought in seven wars under five different flags.

MAJOR WILLIAM MARTIN

In the early morning hours of May 1, 1943, a couple strolling along the Spanish seashore of the Mediterranean Sea suddenly came upon what looked like a piece of rolled clothing mired in the sand at the edge of the surf. Being wartime there had been all kinds of debris washed ashore from damaged ships, or from fallen aircraft, so a discovery of this nature wasn't out of the ordinary. Only, somehow, it looked different. They moved for a closer look and then stopped. It was a body. Not uncommon to see these along the beach either, but this one appeared to be particularly interesting. The body was a high-ranking British officer. They ran to notify the local authorities.

Several Spanish military officials quickly converged on the scene. They searched the body and then wrapped it in a blanket and hauled it up a steep bank and placed it in a truck. Two military guards were placed inside the vehicle as it sped away to a Spanish army building on the outskirts of a small seaside village. Here the wrapped body was unloaded from the truck and whisked behind a heavily guarded door. The ordeal was done so quickly that it aroused little attention from the local populace.

In searching the body, they had come across a document that looked intriguing. It could be a top Allied military secret. Being sympathetic to the Germans, a runner was sent to notify a local German authority, who in turn alerted the German military command. Within hours, German officers had appeared and were carefully examining the water-soaked pages of the document found on the drowned British officer. They couldn't believe their eyes. The contents of the document could change the course of the war in favor of Germany. Hitler had to be notified at once.

Identification revealed the body as being Major William Martin of the British Royal Marines, serial number 09560. On his possession was an envelope that contained papers revealing the Allies next military objective. It was to be an invasion of the Balkans, not Sicily as the Germans had expected. When Hitler was notified of the discovery, he personally took charge of the plans to foil the Allied landings.

The German dictator ordered a crack *Panzer* division from France to head immediately for Greece in order to reinforce his forces already in that area. He then pulled several ships guarding Sicily and deployed them to the waters off southern Greece. And to further bolster his defenses, he had the entire coast line of Greece mined. The Germans would be waiting for them.

On July 10, 1943, more than 467,000 Allied troops stormed ashore on the Italian island of Sicily. There were only 60,000 Germans there to oppose them. The Allied deception had worked and the capture of Sicily was made easier. The door was now opened to invade Italy.

To begin with, back on the night of April 30, the British submarine *H.M.S. Seraph* had silently surfaced a short distance off the Spanish coast. Without a sound, a group of sailors slid the uniformed body, identified as Major William Martin, gently over the side and into the sea, knowing the tide would gradually move it on to the beach. The submarine then quietly slipped beneath the surface and disappeared.

Actually, Major William Martin never really existed. His name, rank and serial number were all fictitious. The important secret documents found on the body were the clever work of British Naval Intelligence. War historians would call the incident one of the most successful deceptions of WWII.

The true identity of the body was never revealed.

IN GOOD HANDS

Several years ago, I was one of many World War II veterans asked to speak to students at a high school about what it was like being in World War II. It was part of the school's Living History Day honoring veterans from all wars. We were each assigned to a classroom where we had an hour to speak, thirty minutes to one group and thirty minutes to another.

After being served a continental breakfast, I was assigned a student guide who took me to my classroom. Sitting in front of me were about forty teenagers, who were at least sixty years younger than I and probably wondering what kind of boring story this old white-haired geezer from the dinosaur age was going to tell them. I couldn't have been more wrong.

At first I wasn't quite sure what they wanted to hear. I told them I had been in the navy in the Pacific attached to a unit called the Navy Armed Guard who served as gun crews aboard merchant ships carrying war supplies. Since nobody had ever heard of the Navy Armed Guard, during or after the war, I thought this might be of special interest to them. Then suddenly I noticed something about a young man that would change my talk entirely.

He was a big kid sitting in the back of the class wearing a baseball cap backwards and sporting a large silver earring in his left ear. I looked around and noticed other boys dressed much the same way. This was really nothing out of the ordinary since the halls were filled with young men that looked much like this. Most had baggy overall pants with the crotch practically dragging on the floor, some had spiked hair, and a few had chains here and there. I noticed some of the girls with either bright blue or orange hair and all wearing jeans. Whatever happened to knee-length skirts, bobby socks and saddle shoes?

I decided to leave the combat stories to the other veterans. I abruptly stopped taking about the war, and asked the young man if his parents approved of how he looked. This was followed by a very heavy silence. Was I out of my mind? This kid could have me for lunch. He finally smiled a little and nodded yes. I then turned to a girl sitting directly in front of me with tattoos running up and down her bare arms. I didn't have to ask her.

"My folks hate these," she said grinning. The class snickered, probably thinking, What business is it of this old guy and what has it got to do with being in a war?

I told them that I was a teenager just like them in 1941 when the war started. It would be a year or so before I would enlist. In the meantime, I was a high school kid doing much the same things they were doing now. We had fads that disturbed our parents, too. This startled them a little, and some doubtful smiles began to creep across their faces. I could imagine them thinking that old folks from a war long ago were never kids that wore dumb stuff and did goofy things.

I told the boys, "You have baggy pants, we had dirty cords. A guy in my time didn't dare go to school with a clean pair of cords." I told them I can remember getting dirt on my hands, then sitting down and rubbing the front of the pants with the dirt so that when I stood up they would have white creases showing through the dirt. I heard a girl's voice quietly say, "Gross," then came, "Cool" from the big kid in the back. I added that much to the dismay of my mother, I could actually stand those cords up in the corner of my bedroom. We twirled chains and wore saddle shoes just like the girls, only ours were kept dirty. The only clean looking part of our attire was a pullover sweater with the sleeves pushed up and a clean shirt underneath. And every guy wore a gray topcoat when it rained. You wouldn't be caught dead wearing a baseball cap to class, let alone backwards.

And what about the girls? I remember long sleeve sweaters with buttons up the front that were turned around and worn backwards. (*They what?*) Then there were those wooden shoes some of them wore that clattered nosily up and down the hallways. (*You're putting us on, right?*) Their skirts were at the knee, they all wore make-up and if they were caught wearing jeans to school they were sent home. (*You got to be kidding!*)

Then I told them about our music. I said I could remember my dad telling me to turn the radio down because what I was listening to was just a "bunch of noise." Sound familiar? I think it was a Benny Goodman big band arrangement. "What's a Benny Goodman?" someone asked. Then there was the dancing. The boy and girl actually embraced each other when the music was slow and dreamy and then they acted like maniacs, throwing each other all over the place when they "jitterbugged" to a swing tune. Today, you have three or four guys banging on amplified guitars and drums and yelling something at you that could burst an eardrum. What did we have? Eighteen musicians blaring their instruments in your face.

They wanted to hear everything. I also told them that as kids we helped with the war effort by doing scrap drives, harvesting crops, giving blood to the Red Cross and taking on extra jobs to replace someone who had to go to war. And before you went to school every morning, you would read the local newspaper to see if anyone you knew had been killed. Once in awhile you did. Then when you graduated, the only choice guys had was going to war, and you did it gladly for your country. When the thirty minutes were up, most of them didn't want to leave the room. Even the next group hung around afterwards, wanting to hear more about being a teenager during the war years.

When the classroom sessions ended at noon, we were all treated to a buffet lunch. Then we lined up and were led to the gymnasium. When they opened the doors, I was completely taken by surprise. Here were more than 3,000 students and their parents waiting for us. As we entered, they gave us a standing ovation that lasted long after we sat down. Then a big dance band made up of students struck up a familiar swing tune from the '40s and jitterbugging kids started filling the aisles. We were stunned. Some of the veteran's couldn't resist the moment and went into the stands and invited teenage girls to come out and dance with them. They were willing, and knew exactly what to do. Suddenly, it was 1941 again. It was one of the most impressive and emotional days of my life.

One week later. I received in the mail a large package containing thank you letters from the students to whom I had talked. When I read them I knew I didn't have to worry. That day, the generation gap had been closed by a bunch of kids whose fads aren't any sillier than the ones we had, and that if given half a chance, are going to take pretty good care of this country.

ABOUT THE AUTHOR

Zed Merrill was born on August 7, 1926 in Albany, Oregon. He enlisted in the U.S. Navy in 1944 and shortly thereafter married Norma Miller, his high school sweetheart. "How apple pie can you get," he remarks, "I was the halfback and she was the drum majorette."

Upon graduating from a Navy signal school, he was enticed to volunteer for the U.S. Navy Armed Guard, a branch of the Navy of which he had never before heard. "We were told it was the best duty in the Navy," he says. "There was no particular dress code aboard ship, we could order our meals from a menu, and we would sleep between sheets. So naturally, I raised my hand. They failed, however, to tell us the true story." This you will read about in the story titled, "The Unknown Navy."

During his time in the Navy Armed Guard, serving as a signalman and part of Navy gun crew aboard a merchant cargo ship, he made three trips into the Pacific delivering war supplies to American fighting forces. He claims the most important signals he ever sent during the war were when his ship would be anchored off some friendly small south sea island and he would be ordered by the gunnery officer to signal ashore, or to a nearby Navy warship, and ask what movie was showing that night so the crew could get invited over to see it.

When the war ended, Zed returned to Albany and went into the advertising and marketing business with his brother, Frank, under the GI bill. In 1954, he and his wife moved to Portland where they raised four daughters and a son while he developed a career as a commercial artist, and later as a television commercial and documentary producer. He also operated his own advertising agency, and before "retiring" at the end of 2002 he had served 14 years as the advertising and marketing director for Elmer's Restaurant, Inc., a popular Northwest family-style restaurant chain.

But it wasn't until 1996, more than fifty years after the war, that he would become aware for the first time that the U.S. Navy Armed Guard had an active veteran's association.

Discovering the Armed Guard veterans group at age 70 gave him a new career at a time when most everybody else his age had long retired. "I found out," he says, "that nobody had ever done a film documentary about the war history of the Navy Armed Guard. That's because nobody had ever heard about us. So I did one."

Zed has produced a number of video documentaries about little-known incidents and military groups pertaining to WWII. All of them have won international awards, appeared on various public television stations and are currently selling by direct-mail and on his website.

Zed and Norma's five children have produced eighteen grandchildren and six great grandchildren. He is quick to add, however, that it was "six when this book went to press."